NEW DEAL DAYS:

THE CCC

AT MESA VERDE

By
Ronald C. Brown
Duane A. Smith

ISBN 1-887805-20-6

Authors
Ronald C. Brown
Duane A. Smith

Mesa Verde Centennial Series Editor
Andrew Gulliford

Content and Copy Editor
Elizabeth A. Green

Design and Layout
Lisa Snider Atchison

Mesa Verde Centennial Series Editorial Committee
Lisa Snider Atchison, Tracey L. Chavis,
Elizabeth A. Green, Andrew Gulliford, Tessy Shirakawa,
Duane A. Smith and Robert Whitson

Printed in Korea

This book is dedicated to Bob and Kathy Heyder
and Jack Smith for their support of history and research
in Mesa Verde National Park. As park superintendent,
Bob organized the first CCC reunion in the 1980s
and encouraged CCCers to attend the Old Timers' picnics.
Jack, who was head of the Research Center in the park
in the 1980s and 1990s, graciously provided absolute
freedom to us as researchers.

A message from the Superintendent of Mesa Verde National Park

Our centennial celebrates an important moment in Mesa Verde National Park's history. It is an opportunity to share stories of what led to establishment of the park on June 29, 1906, and its designation as a World Heritage Cultural Site in 1978. This is a time to reflect upon its past and share hopes and visions for the next 100 years.

As Mesa Verde National Park nears its 100th birthday, it is important to remember that the archaeological sites it protects have been here far longer. Their survival is a credit to the skilled Ancestral Puebloan masons who created them 700 to 1600 years ago.

Following the Puebloan people's migration south to the Rio Grande area around 1300, the Utes continued to occupy the Mesa Verde area. They remain today and were responsible for the protection and preservation of Mesa Verde prior to its establishment as a national park. The park and the American public owe much to all these surviving indigenous people.

More than 100 years before its establishment as a national park, non-native people began exploring and documenting the archaeological sites at Mesa Verde, including Spanish explorers, geologists, ranchers, miners, photographers, naturalists, and archaeologists. They shared the story of fantastic stone cities in the cliffs, attracting more and more visitors to the area.

Prior to 1914, the 25-mile trek from Mancos Canyon to Spruce Tree House took an entire day, traveling the first 15 miles by wagon and the next 10 miles on foot or by horseback. This included a nearly vertical climb to the top of Chapin Mesa. Today more than one-half million people visit Mesa Verde National Park each year – a considerable increase over the 100 visitors documented in 1906.

"Leaving the past in place" is just one of the unique ideas pioneered at Mesa Verde. In 1908, when archaeology mainly consisted of collecting artifacts for distant museums, Jesse Walter Fewkes repaired, but did not rebuild, Spruce Tree House for visitation. He documented the excavation and created a small museum to house its artifacts. That tradition is continued today and Mesa Verde is recognized worldwide as a leader in non-invasive archaeology – studying and documenting sites without shovels to disturb the past. With the involvement of the 24 tribes affiliated with Mesa Verde and ongoing research, we continue to learn more about the stories that Mesa Verde National Park preserves.

Our centennial will celebrate 100 years of preservation and honor all who have gone before us. This centennial book series was created to tell some of their stories, of discovery, travel, transportation, archaeology, fire and tourism. These stories have contributed to our national heritage and reinforce why we must continue to preserve and protect this national treasure for future generations.

Enjoy the celebration. Enjoy the book series. Enjoy your national park.

– Larry T. Wiese

About the Mesa Verde Museum Association

Mesa Verde Museum Association (MVMA) is a nonprofit, 501 (c) 3 organization, authorized by Congress, established in 1930, and incorporated in 1960. MVMA was the second "cooperating association" formed in the United States after the Yosemite Association. Since its inception, the museum association has provided information that enables visitors to more fully appreciate the cultural and natural resources in Mesa Verde National Park and the southwestern United States. Working under a memorandum of agreement with the National Park Service, the association assists and supports various research activities, interpretive and education programs, and visitor services at Mesa Verde National Park.

A Board of Directors sets policy and provides guidance for the association. An Executive Director assures mission goals are met, strengthens partnerships, and manages publishing, education, and membership program development. A small year-round staff of five, along with more than 15 seasonal employees, operates four sales outlets in Mesa Verde National Park and a bookstore in Cortez, Colorado. The association carries nearly 600 items, the majority of which are produced by outside vendors. MVMA currently publishes approximately 40 books, videos, and theme-related items, and more than 15 trail guides.

Since 1996 MVMA has been a charter partner in the Plateau Journal, a semi-annual interpretive journal covering the people and places of the Colorado Plateau. In addition, the association has been a driving force in the Peaks, Plateaus & Canyons Association (PPCA), a region-wide conference of nonprofit interpretive associations. PPCA promotes understanding and protection of the Colorado Plateau through the publication of joint projects that are not feasible for smaller associations.

Mesa Verde Museum Association is also a longtime member of the Association of Partners for Public Lands (APPL). This national organization of nonprofit interpretive associations provides national representation with our land management partners and highly specialized training opportunities for board and staff.

Since 1930 the association has donated more than $2 million in cash contributions, interpretive services, and educational material to Mesa Verde National Park. MVMA's goal is to continue enhancing visitor experience through its products and services, supporting vital park programs in interpretation, research and education

Visit the online bookstore at mesaverde.org and learn more about Mesa Verde National Park's centennial celebration at mesaverde2006.org. Contact MVMA offices for additional information at: telephone 970-529-4445; write P.O. Mesa Verde National Park, CO 81330; or email info@mesaverde.org.

The Center of Southwest Studies

The Center of Southwest Studies on the campus of Fort Lewis College in Durango, Colorado, serves as a museum and a research facility, hosts public programs, and strengthens an interdisciplinary Southwest college curriculum. Fort Lewis College offers a four-year degree in Southwest Studies with minors in Native American Studies and Heritage Preservation. The Center includes a 4,400-square-foot gallery, the Robert Delaney Research Library, a 100-seat lyceum, and more than 10,000 square feet of collections storage. The new $8 million Center of Southwest Studies building is unique among four-year public colleges in the West, because the facility houses the departments of Southwest Studies and Anthropology, and the Office of Community Services, which helps Four Corners communities with historic preservation and cultural resource planning.

The Colorado Commission on Higher Education has recognized the Center of Southwest Studies as a "program of excellence" in state-funded higher education. Recent gifts to the Center include the $2.5 million Durango Collection ®, which features more than eight hundred years of southwestern weavings from Pueblo, Navajo and Hispanic cultures.

The goal of the Center is to become the intellectual heart of Durango and the Southwest and to provide a variety of educational and research opportunities for students, residents, scholars and visitors. Strengths in the Center's collections of artifacts include Ancestral Puebloan ceramic vessels, more than 500 textiles and dozens of southwestern baskets. The Center's holdings, which focus on the Four Corners region, include more than 8,000 artifacts, 20,000 volumes, numerous periodicals, and 500 special collections dating from prehistory to the present and with an emphasis on southwestern archaeology, maps, and original documents. These collections include nearly two linear miles of manuscripts, unbound printed materials, more than 7,000 rolls of microfilm (including about 3,000 rolls of historic Southwest region newspapers), 600 oral histories, and 200,000 photographs. Contact the Center at 970-247-7456 or visit the Center's website at swcenter.fortlewis.edu. The Center hosts tours, educational programs, a speakers' series, and changing exhibits throughout the year.

Center of Southwest Studies website: http://swcenter.fortlewis.edu

About the publisher

The publisher for the Mesa Verde Centennial Series is the Ballantine family of Durango and the Durango Herald Small Press. The Ballantine family moved to the Four Corners region in 1952 when they purchased the *Durango Herald* newspaper.

Durango has a magnificent setting, close to the Continental Divide, the 13,000-foot San Juan Mountains, and the 500,000-acre Weminuche Wilderness. The Four Corners region encompasses the juncture of Colorado, Utah, Arizona, and New Mexico, the only place in the nation where four state borders meet. Residents can choose to ski one day in the San Juans and hike the next day in the wilderness canyons of Southeast Utah. This land of mountains and canyons, deserts and rivers is home to diverse Native American tribes including the Southern Utes, Ute Mountain Utes, Jicarilla Apache, Hopi, Zuni, and the Navajo, whose 17-million-acre nation sprawls across all four states. The Four Corners is situated on the edge of the Colorado Plateau, which has more national forests, national parks, national monuments, and wilderness areas than anywhere else on earth.

Writing and editing the newspaper launched countless family expeditions to Ancestral Puebloan sites in the area, including spectacular Mesa Verde National Park, the world's first park set aside for the preservation of cultural resources in 1906 to honor America's indigenous peoples. The Ballantine family, through the *Durango Herald* and the *Cortez Journal,* have been strong supporters of Mesa Verde National Park and Fort Lewis College.

Arthur and Morley Ballantine started the planning for the Center of Southwest Studies at Fort Lewis College in 1964 with a $10,000 gift. In 1994 Morley began the Durango Herald Small Press, which publishes books of local and regional interest. The Press is proud to be a part of the 100th birthday celebration for Mesa Verde National Park.

Durango Herald Small Press website: www.durangoheraldsmallpress.com

Acknowledgments

Special thanks to Bill Winkler, Don Ross, and Susana Jones for their valuable contributions to this book. Each was asked to research and write about a particular aspect of Civilian Conservation Corps activities in Mesa Verde National Park and did so in a timely, thorough, and readable manner.

Thanks also to the Mesa Verde Museum Association for photos and information related to the museum dioramas built by CCCers. Liz Bauer, of the Mesa Verde Research Center, was very helpful in finding photographs from CCC days in the park.

TABLE OF CONTENTS

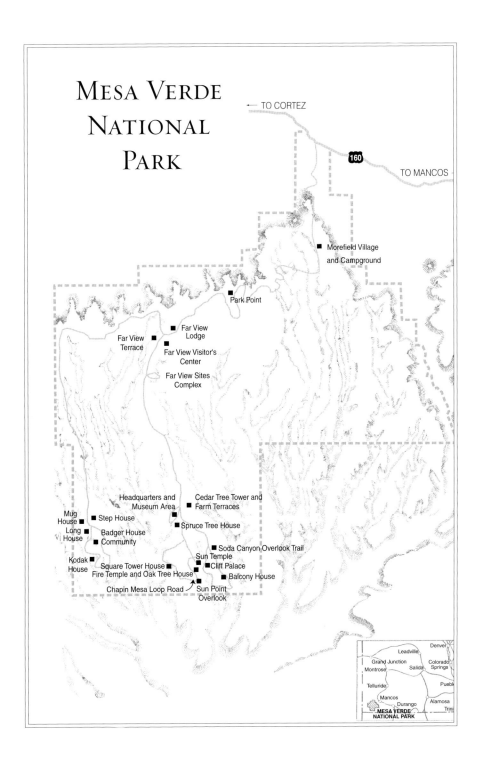

MESA VERDE
NATIONAL
PARK

← TO CORTEZ

160

TO MANCOS

Morefield Village
and Campground

Park Point

Far View
Lodge

Far View
Terrace

Far View Visitor's
Center

Far View Sites
Complex

Headquarters and
Museum Area

Cedar Tree Tower and
Farm Terraces

Mug
House

Step House

Spruce Tree House

Long
House

Badger House
Community

Kodak
House

Soda Canyon Overlook Trail

Sun Temple

Square Tower House

Cliff Palace

Fire Temple and Oak Tree House

Balcony House

Chapin Mesa Loop Road

Sun Point
Overlook

Denver

Leadville

Grand Junction

Salida

Colorado
Springs

Montrose

Telluride

Pueblo

Mancos

Alamosa

Durango

Trini

MESA VERDE
NATIONAL PARK

1932
AMERICA

What will the New Year mean to you? More than ever before, perhaps, the year on which we are about to enter hangs upon initiative, endeavor and shrewdness.

— Durango Herald, January 1, 1931, editorial

Capitalism is, in fact, what we choose to make it. Capitalism is less important than capitalists. The system is one, in essence, which depends upon individual effort, and puts a premium upon success. ... We bid you hope. Let that be the word of cheer, both to old and young on this the first day of the New Year.

— The New York Times, January 1, 1932, editorial

This is the traditional time for business estimates for the New Year. But the prophets are wary now. They have seen too many prophecies fall in these last two years. Business is done with the past. It is ready to face the future and make the best of what hand it draws. Now, with the new deal, we may get somewhere.

— Durango Herald-Democrat, January 1, 1932, editorial

A s 1932 dawned, Americans found themselves locked into a devastating depression that was moving toward its third year. They were not alone in this calamity; the rest of the world, to one degree or another, joined them.

Nor did the term "new deal" strike a familiar chord with many Durango readers, except among the poker players. It would, soon enough.

The golden, bubbling years of the 1920s seemed far removed, as the depression slogged on, grinding down men, women, and children. America had once seemed like the Promised Land, a land where prosperity lay within the grasp of every person. After all, the chairman of General Motors had asserted that all one had to do was save $15 a month and purchase "sound" common stocks. Let the dividends accumulate and after 20 years, the investment would be worth "at least $80,000."

By borrowing today for a better tomorrow, credit put Americans in debt for stocks, cars, homes, and almost everything. Purchasers cheerfully mortgaged their futures to obtain goods that might often be consumed before they could be paid for.

It sounded simple, easy, and nearly foolproof in the heady days of the 1920s stock market bonanza. Unfortunately, several errors existed in such thinking. One of the main flaws was the shaky and overpriced "Great Bull Market," as the booming stock market was fondly called.

Times had never seemed so good, with new products from the radio to "talkies" to better and faster cars. Regrettably, not everyone participated in the "prosperity." Farmers, coal miners, and other workers had not "roared" in the '20s. American prosperity seemingly passed them by.

The end came in October 1929, with a break in stock prices that accelerated downward faster each minute, or so it appeared. "Black Thursday" arrived on October 24. Thousands of small speculators, investors, and brokers were wiped out. The worst panic in stock market history kicked off the "Great Depression." In the last four months of the year, about $40 million in stock values disappeared, along with life savings, jobs, retirement plans, and confidence in the business community and – to a degree – the federal government.

It did not happen all at once. Depression spread throughout the country at varying paces. It hit Durango, for example, in November 1930, when the smelter closed and more than 200 people lost their jobs in a community of 5,400. The shutdown came, banker Rich McComb explained, because of the hard times, which depressed metal prices. He went on to say, "Boy it sure was tough around here. We had a pretty rough go of it and the people who were working – we used to contribute 50 cents or $1 a week" to support less fortunate individuals.

A host of factors besides the stock market caused the crash and depression, but it served as a convenient scapegoat. Initially, American optimism tried to stem the tide.

It did not work, nor did that hit tune of the day, "Happy Days Are Here Again." A few statistics illustrate why. Between 1929 and 1932, industrial production fell by 51 percent and industrial employment by 38 percent. Thirty-two thousand businesses failed in 1932. Farm income had dropped by 50 percent over the past decade and the national income by about half over what it had been only three years before. Banks failed – 5,050 in 1930-1932 alone – carrying with them many depositors' savings, a savage blow.

In more personal terms, by the summer of 1932 at least one out of every four workers in the United States was jobless, perhaps as many as one-third. Slashed paychecks and shortened hours confronted many of the rest. People stood on street corners trying to sell apples. Men walked the streets asking, in the term of the day, "Buddy, can you spare a dime?" Many could not. One of the major problems proved hard to solve: So many of those out of work were young men, with few prospects and limited skills. Recent high school graduate Jim Sartoris remembered those days, "I had nothing to do. You couldn't find work. You couldn't beg, borrow or steal a job."

People lost their homes, farmers their farms, and others their cars and the host of things they had purchased on those ever popular 1920s credit plans. Credit once had promised that all could achieve what they desired. Now debt evened the playing field for not only the poor and lower incomes, but middle-class America found itself engulfed by spreading waves of indebtedness, poverty, and despair as well.

Desperation set in for many Americans, a mood that generated violence. Iowa farmers declared a "holiday" and refused to sell produce while people starved in cities. A march of unemployed workers in Detroit was stopped by bullets and tear gas. World War I veterans marched on Washington, D.C., and set up camps. Revolution? Some conservatives panicked. The marchers were peacefully demanding payment of a veterans' bonus due in 1945, essentially asking for a 12-year advance. Instead, they found themselves forcibly evicted from their camps by the army. So much for the heroes of 1918!

What was it like in the 1930s? Three Durango women reminisced about those days. "We ate corn bread; we were lucky to get corn bread. Dad would bring home a keg of syrup and we ate corn bread," summarized Deora Powell in her memories of those years. For Bessie Finegan that time conjured bittersweet memories better forgotten. "We had a home. We lost it. We couldn't make the taxes, so we just walked out, didn't get a dime out of it."

"Well, if you hadn't anything but squash to eat all winter, you'd eat fast too. "

"There were houses all up and down Third Avenue that were boarded up. People couldn't afford to live in them," recalled Ethel Nelson. She recalled a little boy from across the street who came over for lunch. Her son asked him why he ate so fast. The boy replied, "Well, if you hadn't anything but squash to eat all winter, you'd eat fast too."

Private charity agencies ran out of funds, and cities, counties, and states cut their relief payments, which made it even harder to match the growing needs of the day. Outside of towns and cities, shanty towns of cardboard, tin, and any other castoff materials appeared, proclaiming misery and the failure of the American dream. Folks dug through garbage dumps for food, held jack rabbit roundups to find some meat to eat, offered to do odd jobs in exchange for a meal, and "rode the rails" looking for work.

Those shanty towns gained the appellation "Hoovervilles," and jack rabbits were "Hoover hogs." Both terms symbolized growing disdain for President Herbert Hoover, who seemed powerless to end the economic disaster. Once hailed as a great humanitarian and expert administrator, and admired for his public service, Hoover witnessed his administration, within eights months of his inauguration, fall into the "valley of the shadow of death" and never emerge. Hoover became the convenient scapegoat for the era.

The cheerful words in his 1929 inauguration address turned to ashes. He had forecast that the "poor house" was about to disappear from

America and continued, "In no nation are the fruits of accomplishment more secure. I have no fears for the future of our country. It is bright with hope."

His batting average was zero. Despite some efforts to try to pull the country out of the depression, Hoover and his advisors remained locked into the idea that the business community would save the day. Keep the federal government solvent and let time use its curative powers had been the policy followed since the first economic downturn stalked the new country a century before. Government help to individuals, it was argued, would undermine the American character.

Hoover's administration did move slightly beyond the place that any previous government had ventured, but it all proved too little and too late. By 1932, Hoover's and the Republican Party's reputations hit about the same low as the economy.

Matters came to a head in 1932, a presidential election year. The Republicans, without much fire or enthusiasm, re-nominated Hoover and somehow found the courage to praise his record. The President initially stayed in Washington to help convince the electorate that he was on top of the game, working hard to find the solution. When he finally did campaign, he was greeted in his home state of Iowa with this indignity: "In Hoover we trusted; now we are busted."

The Democrats saw victory on the horizon, especially after their national gains in the 1930 off-year election. They met in Chicago in June and nominated for president the jaunty, optimistic governor of New York, Franklin Roosevelt. The differences between the two men, their campaign styles, and their outlook toward America offered the voters a dramatic contrast.

After flying to Chicago to accept his nomination (the first candidate to personally appear at a presidential convention), Roosevelt dramatically promised, "I pledge you, I pledge myself, to a new deal for the American people." Just what that meant, voters were left to decide, but many of them thought that a new deal seemed to be just what they and the country needed. He worked tirelessly to convince the "forgotten American" that the Democrats had the needed answers.

Roosevelt won 57 percent of the popular vote; for the first time since 1852, the Democrat party had gained the presidency with a popular majority. They swept the field, capturing both houses of Congress as well. It mattered little whether the Republicans had been responsible for existing conditions.

By the time Roosevelt was inaugurated in March 1933, the country had slid farther toward an economic and social abyss, with perhaps as many as 17 million men out of work. The winter of 1932-33 had been the worst yet, and only that confident, serious man who took over the reins of government appeared to block the path to complete disaster. His words that

March 4 seemed to magically restore some of the nation's will.

> This great Nation will endure as it has endured, will revive and will prosper. So first of all, let me assert my firm belief that the only thing we have to fear is fear itself – nameless, unreasoning, unjustified terror which paralyzes needed efforts to convert retreat into advance.

The country, however, had a bit more to fear than fear itself on that March day in '33.

Nevertheless, FDR was about to launch his New Deal, even though perhaps even he did not comprehend where it might be headed. Roosevelt would tinker, change, and experiment to save American capitalism and democracy. One of his most successful experiments was the Civilian Conservation Corps, aimed at those desperate – and often rootless – young men at home and wandering about the country.

1932
MESA VERDE

Attendance at Mesa Verde National Park reflected the mood of Americans about travel. Having fallen head over heels in love with the automobile, they took to the road by the thousands in the '20s. For the first time in its history, Mesa Verde recorded nearly 17,000 visitors in 1928. Worry had surfaced about overcrowding. But by 1932, the number of visitors had dropped to 10,000.

The season usually lasted from mid-May until mid-October, at which point snow made travel into the park treacherous. The route into the park was scary enough anyway, with the "infamous" narrow Knife Edge road confronting drivers.

The '20s belonged to Jesse Nusbaum, the first trained archaeologist to attain the park's superintendency. His presence dominated the decade, and he put his "stamp" on everything. Nusbaum brought the park headquarters into the park, enhanced the museum, improved visitor tours, built the superintendent's home, and saw to it that a small hospital was built to handle tourists' and employees' injuries and illnesses. He upgraded the professionalism of the rangers and accomplished a host of other things as well. By 1929, the tourists' experience had become first-rate.

Then came the summer of 1929. In his annual report for the year, Nusbaum described the tourist season that from the "travel standpoint [was] the most disastrous in the history of the park." In July and August, "disastrous cloudbursts and floods" repeatedly closed Mesa Verde. For the first time since World War I, the number of visitors declined. It foreshadowed, in its own way, the economic drought that was about to dry out the country.

Visitor totals continued downward, except for a brief upswing in 1931. Most of the traffic was local, reported new Superintendent Marshall Finnan, showing the immediate impact on travel to the park. "There has been a decided tendency on the part of the traveling public to see the most economical type of accommodation which has resulted in a material decrease in operators' revenues." Concessionaires, nearby towns, southwestern Colorado – all were hurt.

Park employees endured 8½ percent salary cuts, and construction and maintenance projects took a 10 percent hit. Needed projects were put on hold or delayed indefinitely. So bad were the "financial difficulties," Finnan said in 1932, that he mimeographed his annual report and limited the number of copies prepared.

The Rio Grande Southern Railroad, which so long had dominated visitation to the park, saw its passenger numbers dwindle. Meanwhile, arrivals by automobile went up, with many of the visitors camping along the way and in the park. Construction on, and repairs to, the roads leading to Mesa Verde declined, however, as the depression dragged its way along. And states and counties in the region simply did not have the funds to build or rebuild these vital links which were crucial to the park's prosperity.

As 1932 dawned, Mesa Verde National Park confronted numerous needs, as did the other national parks. The federal government did not have the resources or funds to help, and the future looked none too bright. Visitation continued downward, off six percent from what it had been in 1928.

The decreased budget and financial crisis reached its nadir in 1932-33. As the superintendent observed, "the word economy has risen from obscurity to a prominent place in the thoughts and speech of all Americans."

A cautious mood – one of limited expectations – settled over the country as the "Great Depression" continued unabated. People who could afford little else might be able to take a trip to Mesa Verde. Temporarily, the visitors perhaps could put aside the hard times with a brief vacation, a chance to get away from the reality at their front door. If they had children, the trip would be an educational experience as well.

The park people tried to maintain the quality of the visitors' experience as much as possible. They worked on a shoestring to maintain the buildings and other maintenance. They cleaned up after visitors, prevented vandalism, and anything that needed to be done to at least hold the line until times improved. But here, as elsewhere, times did not improve, and the way ahead looked bleak. The year 1932 seemed the worst yet in all ways and, as it ended, the year 1933 did not promise to be much better. Mesa Verde and the whole park system cried for help. So did the whole country.

INTRODUCTION

W ith nearly a third of the nation's work force unemployed when he took office, President Franklin Roosevelt conceived of an idea: bring young men together throughout the nation; give them work on public lands; shelter, feed, and educate them; and send much of their pay home to their families. From that idea, the Civilian Conservation Corps was created by Congress in the Emergency Conservation Work Act of March 31, 1933.

As it did on public lands throughout the United States, from 1933 until the program was dissolved in 1942, the Civilian Conservation Corps worked in Mesa Verde National Park. In that decade, the young men of the CCC fought a major forest fire, renovated park accommodations for visitors and staff, created a small, visually exciting museum, improved year-round access to the park, removed insect-ravaged deadwood, and landscaped the park headquarters area.

ROOSEVELT'S CCC WAS AN UNUSUAL COLLABORATION AMONG GOVERNMENT DEPARTMENTS: LABOR, WAR, AGRICULTURE, AND INTERIOR.

Though there was no formal agency called the Civilian Conservation Corps until legislation enacted on June 28, 1937, formally renamed the agency, everyone adopted the name that Roosevelt had first chosen. Like many of the New Deal agencies, the Civilian Conservation Corps was routinely referred to by its alphabetical nickname, the CCC. The original act was the ECW. This alphabetical shorthand will be used throughout this discussion of the work done by the CCC in the park.

Some other definitions are also important to the story. The young men enrolled in the CCC were officially described as "enrollees," but contemporaries often referred to them as "the CCCers," "CCC boys" or sometimes simply as "the boys," or "the men." Enrollees joined for a six-month term and were paid $30 per month. From $5 to $8 was paid to the boys as monthly wages and $22-25 was paid to their families back home. Enrollees had to be single males normally between 18 and 25 at the time of enrollment, but several former enrollees asserted that they had been underage when they joined. Most initially came from families on the public relief rolls, but over time other youth joined the CCC. Several later reported that they acquired funds for college or technical education while in the CCC. The camps at Mesa Verde drew their men primarily from Colorado, New Mexico, Oklahoma, and Texas.

Roosevelt's CCC was an unusual collaboration among government departments: Labor, War, Agriculture, and Interior. Labor brought together the recruits, Agriculture and Interior – the so-called Technical Services – assigned and supervised them at work, and War provided their accommodations and took responsibility for them outside work. General administrative oversight resided with the ECW, headed by Robert Fechner (1933-39) and James J. McEntee, his assistant and then successor until its dissolution (1939-42).

Some of the enrollees qualified for appointment as "leaders" or "assistant leaders." Originally 26 were assigned to each camp – eight for the army and 18 for the Technical Services (at Mesa Verde, the park service). These individuals were paid more than the $30 per month that regular enrollees received. Their status as leaders or assistant leaders usually meant that they had skills, whether personal or technical, which set them apart from the unskilled and unemployed youth who formed the vast majority of the CCC. Over time these leaders and assistant leaders were recruited from among the enrollees whose terms were expiring and who had proven to be skilled, hard-working, natural leaders.

The CCC camps also employed so called "locally experienced men" usually abbreviated L.E.M. or LEMs. At Mesa Verde LEMs were carpenters, plumbers, bricklayers, quarrymen, road construction supervisors, mechanics, foresters – skilled workers who oversaw the CCC work crews and their labor. Each CCC camp had three military officers: the company commander, the assistant commander who handled personnel records, and the company physician. Normally, but not always, U.S. Army officers or army reservists filled these positions.

During a third of the CCC's nine-year existence at Mesa Verde, from July 1934 to October 1937, there were two companies of enrollees, each with its own staff and camp. Each camp had a civilian project superintendent who reported to the park service superintendent. James W. Townsend and J.J. "Pop" Drennan were the senior project superintendent and project superintendent, respectively, of the camps from 1934 to 1937. When fully staffed, a CCC camp had 200 enrollees, but the Mesa Verde camps rarely had more than 180 during any month.

The Labor Department recruited the enrollees and transported them to army stations where they were classified, organized into units, and then transported to the places where they would be put to work. Normally the men sent to Mesa Verde National Park arrived in Mancos via the railroad and disembarked for transportation by truck to their campsite in the park. Initially, specific military training was limited to such activities as reveille, roll call, barracks inspections and KP for disciplinary reasons.

In instructions dated March 27, 1933, the Eighth Corps Area headquartered at Ft. Sam Houston, Texas, (Mesa Verde's Corps Area) explained, "The Corps will be organized under officers of the Regular Army into units appropriate to the sub-divisions of the shelter available." Army personnel selected for this duty were expected to avoid "hard-boiled methods in management or discipline" and cautioned against the unnecessary use of military terms. The instructions explained that the purpose for this low-key approach was "to prevent adverse criticism toward the regular army which will be advanced by pacifists and communists who will be in the ranks of this corps and who will use or invent pretexts to advertise the fact that the regular army is using these unfortunate people to augment the trained man-power of the nation."

After the enrollees reached the army station, the officers made a preliminary examination of them to insure that they had no obvious physical or mental disabilities. Those who did could be rejected on the spot. The others were moved to a camp or post where they were given a complete mental and physical examination. If they were not rejected there, then they would be inoculated for smallpox, typhoid, and paratyphoid. Any individuals whose physical or mental condition kept them from performing "ordinary labor" or who might constitute a menace to the health and welfare of the organization were to be rejected and transported to the place of their initial recruitment into the corps.

Each enrollee had to sign an oath of enrollment, attesting to the accuracy of the information he had provided and agreeing to remain in the Civilian Conservation Corps for the designated enrollment period – six months.

OATH OF ENROLLMENT
(FORM 1 – 1933)

I, _____, do solemnly swear (or affirm) that the information given above as to my status is correct. I agree to remain in the Civilian Conservation Corps for six months unless sooner released by proper authority, and that I will obey those in authority and observe all the rules and regulations thereof to the best of my ability and will accept such allowances as may be provided pursuant to law and regulations promulgated pursuant thereto. I understand and agree that any injury received or disease contracted by me while a member of the Civilian Conservation Corps cannot be made the basis of any claim against the Government except such as I may be entitled to under the act of September 7, 1916 (39 Stat. 742) [an act to provide compensation for employees of the United States suffering injuries while in the performance of their duties and for other purposes], and that I shall not be entitled to any allowances upon release from camp, except transportation in kind to the place at which I was accepted for enrollment. I understand further that any articles issued to me by the United States Government for use while a member of the Civilian Conservation Corps are, and remain, property of the United States Government and that willful destruction, loss, sale or disposal of such property renders me financially responsible for the cost thereof and liable to trial in the civil courts. I understand further that any infraction of the rules or regulations of the Civilian Conservation Corps render me liable to expulsion therefrom. So help me God.

Once these young recruits entered the CCC, they lived in camps administered from dusk to dawn and on weekends and holidays by U.S. Army officers. The daily work of the CCC boys in the Mesa Verde camps was overseen by park service personnel.

Newly recruited enrollees normally were withheld from actual work under the Technical Services for two weeks after their first arrival in camp. During this time they were given general instruction about camp life and learned to arrange their belongings. New enrollees spent this time qualifying for vacant skilled positions such as truck drivers or other positions that required special skills. All new enrollees were examined so as to determine their eligibility to undertake the exacting physical labor that would be required of them.

Normally untrained new recruits found themselves preparing for fieldwork that required simple tools such as shovels and saws. One of the few exceptions to this practice occurred during the Mesa Verde fire of 1934, when newly arrived men from Company 1843 were quickly processed and then sent to a temporary camp near the fire site. By contrast, men transferred from other CCC camps went immediately into the field. For this reason the project superintendents were always delighted to receive winter transfers from summer camps such as the one in Pagosa Springs.

In typical army fashion, the local CCC units were organized into companies with numeric designation and they resided in specific camps. The earliest CCC recruits reached Mesa Verde National Park on May 27, 1933. This camp was designated NP-2-C, an abbreviation which stood for National Park, camp number 2, in Colorado. It was a "summer" camp headquartered in Prater Canyon, just past the modern tunnel separating the campground from the canyon. The first enrollees lived and ate in canvas tents, subject to the extremes of life on the Mesa Verde. They had joined during the first six-month enrollment period which began on April 1, 1933, and ended on September 30, 1933, though Camp NP-2-C did not cease operations until October 31, 1933.

Shortly after the beginning of the third enrollment period (April 1-September 30, 1934), Company 861 arrived to reoccupy Camp NP-2-C. This company received authority to continue as a "winter" camp, and remained at Mesa Verde National Park until its dissolution in 1942. During its eight-year history, Company 861 would occupy all of the CCC camps in the park (NP-2-C, NP-6-C, and NP-5-C where the rec hall and a CCC barrack still stand). Senior Project Superintendent James W. Townsend arrived with Company 861 and served until its dissolution in 1942.

On July 19, 1934, Mesa Verde got its second permanent CCC unit, Company 1843, which was one of the drought relief camps created by the

Roosevelt administration in 1934. Project Superintendent J.J. Drennan supervised the work of Company 1843. Though it too was lodged briefly at Camp NP-2-C, it also was authorized as a winter camp in 1934 and its permanent camp was designated DNP-5-C, with the "D" standing for its status as a Drought unit. During 1934 the Roosevelt administration requested, and Congress authorized, an expansion of the CCC to assist with drought relief associated with the Dust Bowl of the mid-1930s. After the fourth enrollment period (October 1, 1933 - March 31, 1934) the "D" was dropped from the camp number. From that point forward there were no distinctions between the companies, although Superintendent Drennan noted that Company 861 had both more and more varied projects than did his Company 1843.

The permanent camps for Companies 861 and 1843 were built just north of the park service headquarters on Chapin Mesa. The approval of the two winter camps at Mesa Verde brought dramatic improvements in the conditions that the enrollees experienced during their service in the park. Both had wood frame barracks, which were heated by coal-fueled stoves and ventilated by parallel rows of windows along the long sides of the rectangular buildings. Both camps had wooden latrines and showers, as well as mess and recreation halls. The camps were connected by a road near the juncture of which was the ECW utility area, the park reservoir, and the deep well. Though relatively close in proximity, the two companies functioned independently most of the time. Each had its own programming, camp newspaper, and even its own weekly menus.

During the time that the two companies successively operated from the original campsite in Prater Canyon, they worked on projects nearby. Company 1843 spent much of summer 1934 working on the infamous Knife Edge road and built damage control check dams in Prater Canyon. Contemporary reports criticized the location for its heat in summer, cold in fall, and unsatisfactory water and sanitation situations. The CCCers in both companies rejoiced when they relocated to their permanent camps by the Spruce Tree House. Most CCCers lived here while they worked in Mesa Verde National Park.

Visitors can observe the legacy of the Mesa Verde CCC Companies 861 and 1843 along the trails and roadways of the park, in the rock work around the headquarters, or in the less frequented old campground and campfire ring. The enrollees spent many days working on the old road along the Knife Edge, and modern visitors can view remnants of the infamous road by walking to it from the Morefield Village campground or looking back toward it from the auto pull-off at the Montezuma Valley Overlook. Now a fourth generation of Americans is learning about the CCC through the centennial project and through various exhibits and ranger programs developed over the past quarter century. Probably 3,000 to 4,000 CCCers passed through Mesa Verde in the program's nine-year history; their work has enriched the experiences of millions who have come as visitors.

I

THE CCC BOYS
TELL THEIR STORIES

"I didn't mind it too much, I lived through it, so did everyone else."

T he saga of the young men who served in the Civilian Conservation Corps at Mesa Verde can best be told in their own words. Even decades later, their experiences remained fresh in their minds as they discussed their days in the park. A time of youth, of fun and work, a time to have a job, a time to get away from the crushing realities of the 1930s depression, a time to make a contribution to the past, present, and future – it was a never-to-be-forgotten experience.

Fortunately Mesa Verde recognized the significance of their experiences and established an oral history program. From that program and from other interviews collected by the authors, their stories emerge, stories of a moment in time not so long ago.

Two friends discussed their CCC days at Mesa Verde and what the CCC meant to them. John McNamara, who was a Durango student prior to his CCC enrollment, was grateful for the work.

> I enjoyed – well at the time I didn't, it was just like everything else. But darn I was happy because one time I went down Main Street – and every damn store both sides of the street – and said I would work for $10 a week. And I didn't get one [job]. I was tickled to get in there.

After his stint in the CCC, McNamara returned to Durango, eventually becoming a partner in an electric company. Coyne Thompson, who later became a claims adjuster in Durango, concurred with McNamara's assessment of the CCC.

> You couldn't get a job because people, like on the farms, could not afford to feed you, so you couldn't work for room and board. 1930-34 were the bad years.

Herb Hawkins was blunt about joining the CCC. "Back in those days you went to the CCCers or you lived with your folks. But if they were so dad-burned poor you went to the CCC. That was a godsend."

Hawkins went on to explain, "We knew nothing about the CCCers; I came from Oklahoma." He recalled that most of the "people came from Texas and Oklahoma and a few locals. A few Spanish were from Colorado." ("Spanish" was used at that time to describe anyone who spoke Spanish, whether they were American-born or not.)

Thompson had a slightly different view, probably because he was local. A CCC boy's perspective on where his co-workers came from apparently depended on when he worked at Mesa Verde and even what barrack he lived in.

There were a bunch of fellows in the camp from Cortez, and Mancos, and Dolores. They picked up all the slack guys locally to begin with and finally there was a group that came in from Pueblo and they were a rowdy outfit, really rowdy. There were not many outsiders to begin with, San Juan Basin mostly.

Robert Beers lived in Mancos and worked on CCC projects for the summer before his senior year in high school. "They took a bunch of us up there – all my friends – and we stayed up there until we came back in time to go back to school." Beers later settled in Durango, where he became president of Basin Petroleum and served as mayor.

Regarding who appeared in the camps, Jim Holston made an interesting observation. "Some of the boys had a choice of going to the CCCers or going to the pen. It was a way to get them out of and away from [their] environment." He went on to say, however, there were "no discipline problems when I was in there."

Walter Goff, who worked with the CCC in various capacities, observed "that most of the boys were from the streets from Denver and everywhere else." Then he added, "they knew very little about working," but in his estimation "were very well restricted."

A potpourri of jobs awaited the CCCers as they arrived at Mesa Verde. Even at the tail end of the CCC days, 1941, Camp Commander A.D. Brewer listed a variety of tasks his boys were doing. "Work time," he recalled, "involved building trails, ruin restoration, building benches, and making signs." Some CCC crews put in a telephone at his camp, recalled Herman Wagner.

"I worked on the well; I was a pumper," said Jim Holston. Water continued to be a problem on the dry mesa, and not just for its scarcity. "That well was over a mile deep. That water was so hot you could take a bath in it when it came out. That's why they had a sprinkler system, to help cool it down."

> I went up there at night, round the clock we pumped all the time, we transferred from [one] tank to another. I kept things going. I'd keep the things going. We had a tank for the CCC boys at our camp, and another tank for [Company] 861. We pumped water for the headquarters and all that.

Finally, the park quit using the well. "I think it was too expensive. There were quite a bit of repairs." Holston also recalled those snowy days when the park was closed, as it was from fall to spring. The CCC boys drove the dump trucks which hauled snow, and dirt and rocks regularly. "We loaded the trucks with shovels." Herman Wagner drove a dump truck, among a variety of things he did in the park.

I drove a dump truck hauling dirt into the headquarters loop. Work was being done on the parking lot, landscaping the grounds around the museum and the headquarters loop. I hauled the dirt and then it was spread out. The dirt was loaded into the dump truck with a small gas shovel. The CCC was using park service equipment at that time – shovels, and cats and dump trucks. While I was driving the truck I was supervised by park employees.

Driving a truck could be a scary proposition. "I was on the trucks," Herb Hawkins pointed out. "I hauled everything. You always had slides on Knife Edge. So many CCC people were assigned there. Once it slid, out you went. In the winter time about half your time was out there. Gosh it was narrow."

Speaking of those trucks, "we had a full-time night mechanic and day mechanic. The CCC boys worked at night year-round [in the garage]. They worked until midnight at the garage unless [there was an] emergency snowstorm and [then] they worked on. If things happened to a truck during the day, they would fix it at night."

Kenny Ross went to Mesa Verde with the CCC as a Local Experienced Man. "I went up there mainly to work on the exhibits [see chapter on dioramas]." He recalled some of his experiences in a July 1986 interview in which he stressed how the "CCC boys" helped out Mesa Verde.

> The campfire circle as we called [it] on the rim of the canyon, was built by them. All the curbing work at the headquarters and elsewhere was built by the CCC. They did an awfully lot of the road maintenance, not on the highway, and helped remarkably with the museum work.

As for the weather, Ross remembered the "autumns, you can't beat them."

After relying on "just a big generator" to power the radios and lights, the park finally got electricity thanks to the Rural Electrification Administration. That brought back a fond memory of his CCC days and later work as a park ranger.

> That was an experience in the late thirties and early forties to see the lights go on all over the country. Driving back and forth it was very striking. It happened over a period of many months, first a light way out by Pleasant View, then another blinks on somewhere else. It was interesting, you realized something was going on, the country was moving out of the real pioneering life into the modern world.

Camp commander A.L. Brewer, reminisced about the time a mudslide caused more grief than usual. Trucks, boys, perhaps a steam shovel or grader raced to clear the road. That particular time, however, the slide had a longer impact. "The old Knife road was in use and there were times when there were mudslides. One time some VIPs were up here on an inspection tour. A big mudslide came and we were marooned up here for four days. To get those people back they had to hike back over the mountain. That stirred up work for a new road."

In those days before environmental concerns, mud simply was pushed over the side, with an exception. Brewer explained, "they were afraid to push too much of that mud over the road for fear that it would pull down the road."

Besides driving the dump truck, Herman Wagner helped spruce up the park. "I carried trash and tree limbs from the side of the road so that tourists couldn't see it." He also cleared brush away from under the power lines.

Animals sometimes caused the CCC boys grief. Brewer described what some skunks managed to do. "There was a family of skunks that got down in the basement. By park service rules they could not kill them and they had quite a time trying to get them out of there."

Maybe they could not kill skunks, but porcupines were another matter. Bob Beers briefly worked on the porcupine crew. "They had quite an invasion of porcupines. The job of the porcupine crew was to go out and shoot 'em. It was devastating; they were after tree after tree. I've never seen anything like it. I was on it a short time and liked it except we had to get up when it was dark to get started."

John McNamara remembered it slightly differently. "We went out at night with flashlights to kill porcupines. There were a hell of a slug of them and they were just ruining the trees. They would eat around the trunks." Wagner, who also helped with the "porcupine elimination crew," concurred, "lots of trees were damaged by the porcupines."

Beers was not particularly fond of getting up early. One of the army officers "could hardly speak English and he would come by when I was [on] the porcupine crew and hit your bunk to wake us up and say, 'porcupine man; up, porky.' So we got up to shut him up."

Getting up early paled in comparison to one task "given" to some of the boys by A.L. Brewer. "The latrine was quite run-down when I came up here and it was one of my projects to restore that thing. It was pretty terrible."

Among other things, his crew worked on improving and repairing the trails. The CCCers also worked on making signs and benches and knocking down overhangs along the road and over Cliff Palace. Making the park as safe as possible was also a park service and CCC goal.

CCC boys helped build the ever popular dioramas located in the museum. Under the guidance of Don Watson, they got caught up in this fascinating and time-consuming project. Watson had the boys do background "rock work and the figures, animals and like that." CCCers also cataloged the library collection and archaeological material and helped reconstruct pottery from potsherds.

"I worked on landscaping; I put all these trees in the park. I guess we had about 30 fellows working on landscaping at [one] time." Joe Espinoza believed he and his fellows got into planting and landscaping "because we were farmers." In the winter "we used to take down the dead trees."

He also worked on the trail "down to Spruce Tree House." Over the time he worked in the park, Espinoza handled a variety of other jobs including working around Sun Temple and fighting the "big fire" – actually two fires, the first of which started July 9, 1934, and burned into the second two days later – on Wetherill and Wickiup mesas. As he later said, "we worked everywhere."

Meredith Guillet helped fight the 1934 Wetherill Mesa fire. He had not even had time to officially sign up as a CCCer when he and three others were sent out. Not belonging to any crew, he felt "nobody wanted us. They didn't have food for the ones they had."

We started down there and saw spot fire burning and no one there had much experience working fires. We stopped and wondered what they had done leaving all these fires burning behind them. We started putting out the spot fires. When we finally got to the fire, they were bringing sandwiches over by horseback. We hadn't had anything to eat until we finally took some cheese and bread.

The firefighters camped at what someone with a humorous bent named "Camp Filthy McNasty." Eventually help arrived to the isolated crews when "they bulldozed the roads so they could get the trucks down there."

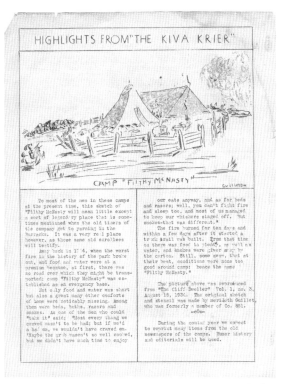

Kiva Krier **1934 with a cartoon by Guillet illustrating "Camp Filthy McNasty."**

Guillet did remember one amusing episode in the otherwise serious situation. "One of the CC truck drivers backed into our beans and spilled those beans all over the place." At the time, however, they probably were more upset than amused.

The CCC firefighters found themselves short of equipment. Jackson Clark, whose father owned Jackson Hardware in Durango, recalled that July. "I remember my dad went down to the store and got ropes, buckets, axes and loaded them in the pickup. They bought everything we had in the store, and took it up to the park."

Herb Hawkins really wanted to drive a truck. "Every fellow, I suppose, who ever went to the CCCers wanted to be an equipment operator or a truck driver." He got his wish, but not quite like he might have hoped.

> I finally got a truck driving job. But I had never driven a truck in my life. I thought there would be a period for instruction. We had to take a driver's test; the first day out we were driving a truck at the Knife Edge. There had been a slide and we were dumping rocks over the edge. The driver I was with – we were supposed to work together for 10 days – said he would take it in the morning, I would in the afternoon. Then he said he would not be back tomorrow as he had a better job. It paid $6 a day. I said I had never driven a truck in my life. He said, "keep your damn mouth shut; I got to get out of here tomorrow." I dumped my first load in the middle of the road, but I finally learned how.

He survived, as they all did, and came away with skills that he could use throughout the rest of his life. That was one of the pluses of the Civilian Conservation Corps at Mesa Verde and elsewhere.

"Very few of these young men have had an opportunity to learn a trade," former park ranger Robert Coates observed. In 1933, as a landscape foreman, he worked in "close contact with the boys." In the CCC plan, "as far as possible they are given an opportunity to do work they prefer in effort to help them become better qualified for that work."

Coates went on to say, "When the boys entered the camp they listed the type of work they would prefer." With what must have been a chuckle, he noted, "no one expressed a desire to learn any of the intricacies of pick and shovel operation." Indeed, one interesting answer was "No work – baseball"! That young man, Coates remarked, played "plenty of baseball but not until his day's work is completed."

John McNamara recalled what happened after he participated in an incident in Dolores that involved putting the local jail in the river. He was assigned to an "infamous" work crew for his part in the escapade.

> So I got put on what they called the Perkins gang. They were

obliterating the old, old road. These two guys, Perkins and Donny, were the bosses and they were regular chain gang bosses, I tell you. You stopped five minutes to get a drink of water twice a day. I was pretty young and I took it.

Regarding discipline, Camp Commander A.L. Brewer felt problems only happened occasionally, and there were "not too many discipline problems....Once in awhile one came in drunk" and he had one CCCer during his brief tenure who "left here on a snowy night."

Robert Beers also worked in the office after working outside in other jobs. He was none too happy about the transfer. "They found out somehow that I knew how to run a typewriter, so I got stuck in the office" typing those innumerable New Deal reports. "I ran the typewriter, primarily payroll type information, and jobs accomplished. It was very dull and I was fuming all the time. All my friends were out having a hell of a good time, shooting porcupines."

Beers also worked on the "bug crew" and had a tough go of it.

> This was an invasion, I think probably they call it the bud worm; they infect trees and kill trees. We would find an infected tree, cut it down, cut it up, and drag it off. Way off somewhere and burn it. It was awfully hard work; it was pretty tough. That was a tough one and I was glad to get off that.

Herb Hawkins was one of those fighting insects that were killing the trees. "I was working cutting these bug trees. Boy that was another thing. I couldn't understand why we had to pick up every chip, everything and take it away and destroy it. That was the way you could control the bugs in the park."

There was a reason for this careful collection of all bits and pieces. Fearing spread of the infestation, the CCC had the boys carefully saw the trees. Then they cut the limbs off, peeled the bark to expose the bugs, piled everything up and burned the lot. Working with the insects and dead trees left the boys with less than fond memories.

Hawkins elaborated on getting rid of those diseased and dead trees, usually during the winter "when the snow was deep."

> There might be one dead tree that you would isolate. The big stuff would be hauled away and the small stuff would be burned; that was how they got rid of the bug. We would haul trees to the dump and burn them. They were called tree monkeys. There would be one tree monkey for each tree around that fire to be sure it would not go where it wasn't supposed to go. If it was necessary you would stay all night. We took out more pine than we [did]

pinyon, [because] they were more infected. We [would] put diesel oil over the whole area then leave it until it was all saturated. You didn't burn it immediately. Then you would burn the whole works; then you were there until it didn't smolder anymore. Another crew put in grass or something.

Life might have seemed "tough," but there were always those moments that provided a good laugh. Beers remembered one as his crew was going to work.

We scared up a bobcat. Most of us were in the back of the truck. He ran across the road and made a mistake; he went up that real steep [shale] bank – loose gravel and the whole nine yards. He got up near the top, and I never shall forget, the guy driving saw him and stopped. One of the guys with us had his bean shooter, slingshot. That animal was within three or four feet of the top and just working pretty hard, couldn't get up. The guy pulled up with his bean shooter and hit him right on the rear end. He jumped all the rest of the way. I shall never forget that scene in my life.

The CCC also did rock work at the headquarters. John McNamara described his experience.

They built the stone works at the headquarters. It was quarried out of sandstone, cut in blocks and hauled to headquarters. The parking lot and all that you see at headquarters was made by the CCC. I worked on that for a while. They would drill holes, put steel wedges and double jack it out. About 20 of us at a certain command would swing and it only took a couple of swings before the whole block fell out. The stonemasons who were members of the camp would cut them into blocks. Then we would load it on trucks.

While they worked a full day, life in camp took up most of their time. Herman Wagner lived in "tents in Prater Canyon" about "a mile down the canyon from the old Knife Edge road." His memory of the camp tells much about the 1933 CCC.

We had a mess tent, cook's "cabin," and living quarters for the men which were tents with bunks in them. There were no wooden buildings at the time. There were 15 to 20 men, at least, per tent. We cooked with a coal stove. The camp's trash was hauled off. The camp was not set up to go through the winter.

Wagner did not have to face the winter; he was discharged in September to return to high school. Despite living and working in the national park, he said his group "did not visit any of the ruins, except maybe Spruce Tree House on a lunch break."

Lunch was brought to the workers in the field. Jim Holston delivered lunches one summer to the "guys working in Morefield Canyon building a fire road."

> I hauled lunches in a pickup with insulated big thermos bottles. It was hot lunches, you set it up down there just as you would in camp. There was coffee and everything else. It was the same meal they had in camp. Oh, we had sometimes steaks at noon, spaghetti, chicken whatever the mess sergeant made up [for] the menu – salads, cakes, bread, desserts.

As for the food, Bob Beers remembered "it was passable." He described cleaning up at the end of a meal.

> They had a couple of big sort of tubs with boiling water and you went to the first one and scraped off anything you didn't eat and go on to the second one and slush it [plate] around. It smelled like lye – I don't know what it was – and then you went to the third one and rinsed it off.

Beers went on to say, "Every meal we had, particularly the noon meal, it was so hot. We'd stand in line right by where they were heating all this water and it was so hot it was miserable."

Segregation in the camp at Mesa Verde was typical for the day and time. During Jim Holston's days there "Barrack three was all Spanish, the rest of them all white. Both Spanish and whites worked in the cook house." Herb Hawkins said the same about his camp. "They had one barrack all to themselves. Just that one barrack that had Spanish."

Holston described the camp detail for those preparing the food: "Some cook had to be on duty all the time, seven days a week. They had four or five cooks and had a baker and a relief for him. They had a mess sergeant."

The camp was run like a military operation and Holston vividly recalled that experience. "They came in and inspected our bunks every day just like in the army. You had to make your bunk up and sweep and scrub every day. The trash was hauled out to the park service dump every day and buried." However, permanency was not one of the required goals for their living quarters. "The barracks were not put up to last forever. They were built to knock the wind off. They had two great big stoves in each one. Heated them up pretty good. They burned coal."

Hawkins elaborated, "We had two rows of beds and two huge stoves. The barrack leader lived in there; he had to, to keep control." One barrack in his camp was divided with the cooks at one end. "It was partitioned off. When the guard came in to wake them [cooks] up, they did not want to wake up everybody."

"We had uniforms similar to the army. All that wool, scratchy stuff – that was our uniform. Just like the army – tie, shirt, pants," Hawkins reminisced. "We had denim for summer and work. Everybody had a set of clothes for work and dress. You were given one uniform and if it wore out you had to pay for a second."

"The barracks were good," Bob Beers said. "They weren't too crowded and I was on an upper bunk." Nevertheless, there "were not enough showers. Sometime we had to wait quite a bit." Like others, he mentioned that he was "furnished some clothes and a blanket, and I think a pillow."

In several other ways it was similar to military life. Laundry was done for the CCCers. But Herb Hawkins worried about inspections. "We had inspection on every Saturday morning and you would be graded on everything. Boy, would it be socked to you. I shined my truck; I thought it had to be perfect."

Jim Holston explained further about camp life. While they did not go through "military drill, it was kind of like the military. We had colors every morning and reveille every evening. We had military surplus clothes to wear and in the evening, before our evening meal, we lowered the flag. We had to go out and stand retreat." Holston described his camp in detail.

> We had a circle drive and our flag set right in the middle of it. There was a garage for our truck and barracks. A cooks' barrack and on around was the mess hall, latrine, and shower room. In the recreation court we played ball, volleyball. The administration building was partitioned. The east end was the sick bay, then the captain's office. The first sergeant's office and the lieutenant's office were on the other side. The doctor's and officers' quarters were up there too. There was no water in the barracks; there was water in the latrine and in the mess hall.

One of the goals of the CCC was to improve the health of the men in the camps. Each camp had "sick call every morning." Holston related that, "we were quarantined one time when someone showed up with chicken pox or something." Overall, though, Mesa Verde's health record seems to have been outstanding.

When he arrived to be the camp commander A.D. Brewer was not impressed by what he found. "The latrine was quite run-down ... the mess was terribly run-down. It was pretty terrible. There were not enough utensils for serving bowls and they would all be dipping in with their own utensils. It was not too sanitary." One source of food was rather interesting. "If deer were killed on the highway, they would bring it up here, cool it and butcher it out." He went on to add "not in my time, however; I heard about it."

Despite all that and adding that "I don't want to talk about some of it," Brewer enjoyed his short time there. "We had not been married too long. We lived in this cluster of houses that were furnished by the park service. We had fireplaces and the Indians would bring in coal."

At the end of the day, Coyne Thompson explained, "you'd get cleaned up for chow and then the time was yours until time to go to bed. We signed out at 9." For that end of the day, various things were available – some in camp, some outside. Hawkins commented, "You had a px book of checks and you could go to the px to buy what ever you wanted. The px was in the mess hall." Some called it a canteen, and apparently part of the time they could charge their "smokes and candy." Others enjoyed walking or other recreational opportunities, and each camp had a library.

For budding reporters and the literarily-inclined, the Mesa Verde camps published newsy papers. Initially Company 861 produced the *Kiva Krier*, while Company 1843 produced the *Mesa Verdian*. On Christmas Day, 1935, the two papers were merged into a single publication, the *Cliff Dweller*. In August 1936 Conrad Wirth, assistant director of the park service, commended Superintendent Jesse Nusbaum on the "very creditable little paper." As to the origins of the papers, Wirth had actually requested copies of camp newspapers and so it may be assumed that they had been recommended by ECW.

The Mesa Verde basketball team had no place to practice or play, so they had to go to Cortez to use the high school gym, a 60-mile round trip. Mesa Verde also fielded a softball team which the *Kiva Krier* (August 15, 1933) proudly reported beat Durango 11-3. Softball and baseball games between teams from the various barracks became quite spirited at times.

Speaking of the evening hours, John McNamara enjoyed a particular card game. "Jawbone poker comes from writing it down who owes this or that. Then at the end of the month you better settle up or you got the name of a welcher. That wasn't a good deal."

He had another experience during his CCC days. "I was taught boxing at Mesa Verde; thought I was pretty damn good. Then one night I mixed it up pretty good and I was on my back in about a minute."

A lot of the CCC boys used to shoot a lot," Jim Holston recalled and he thought "they had a rifle range." Looking back, some wintertime amusements came to mind.

> It was wintertime and no one could go to town. We went over to the quarry and got some tin and folded it into toboggans. We went right over the canyon; it is a miracle we did not kill our-

selves, but we had to do something. It was a pretty fast time; I think they are still down there.

He went on to relate, "In the evening they had movies in the rec hall. On Friday night they'd bring us to town to go to the movie or dance. They'd wait and we'd catch the truck to go back." These movies included such all-time National Park Service favorites as "*Beavers, Glimpses of Yosemite, High Roads to Sky Roads,* and *Natives of Glacier.*"

If possible on weekends, the CCCers tried to get to Mancos, Cortez, or Durango. McNamara explained, "Whenever we could go to Durango we would. Somebody's dad would drive us back; not many kids that age had cars. There were a few cars but not many." Coyne Thompson agreed, "not many at all."

With $25 of their monthly salary going back home or into a government required savings account, the boys were left with $5 per month. That was not the hardship it might seem today because $5 went further in those days. Jim Holston explained, "You had money to go to the movies; a show only cost a dime. Haircuts were 25 cents, candy bars were a nickel, cigarettes were 15 cents or a nickel. A lot of the guys rolled their own cigarettes, the older fellows." He also pointed out that some of "the boys' families sent some of the money back to them."

Thompson recalled how he spent his pay. "You know with that $5 we did an amazing amount of things. We would come in here [Durango] to a dance, dances were down at the old Belmont hall, the old Oliger building – the floor is on boxcar springs. That was the only entertainment, was a dance on Saturday night. Everybody geared up to go to the dance."

John McNamara elaborated, "You paid 10 cents a ticket to dance. You could go down there singly; there were always a bunch of stag girls there or you could take a date."

Joe Espinoza remembered a variation of those weekly dances. "We used to have dances up here. We had CCC trucks go get the girls from Cortez. We behaved pretty good; sure I behaved...I did. About 75 to 100 people would show up." He then added an interesting tidbit, "they used to have beer up here until somebody got hurt." "Our entertainment? We might have a movie once a week, usually on Friday," added Herb Hawkins.

The *Mancos Times-Tribune,* October 5, 1934, commenting on those dances at Mesa Verde, reported "the younger set attended the CCC dance." It was a "housewarming affair" for the new quarters near the headquarters and the Belmont orchestra furnished the music. "Over 100 tickets" were sold and the youngsters had an "enjoyable time." The paper also carefully noted that chaperones went with "each truck" from Mancos.

John McNamara recalled one episode with a twinkle in his eye and a chuckle in his voice.

I went to Dolores one time with a bunch of guys to a dance. I had been working in the office taking a dictation, and typing. Then I went to this dance and the Dolores guys didn't think much of that; the girls liked it, but anyway there was big donnybrook and I just sat back and watched it. I was more of a lover than fighter, but I got in a couple of them. They threw a couple of guys in jail. The guys that were on that truck went over and picked up the jail, lifted it off its foundation and put it in the Dolores River. We got the guys out and went home. As you can imagine, there was quite a stink raised about it.

Sometimes CCC boys got into a fight which led to sporting entertainment. Hawkins looked back to those events.

What they would do if you got in a fight, instead of having this movie, they would take these two involved in the fight down to the mess hall. And there was this stage-like thing at one end and they would put them on the stage with gloves. No such thing as three minute rounds, they would fight until one fell down or had to quit.

Some of the local ranchers and farmers were none too fond of their daughters being seen with these "strangers," the Mesa Verde CCC boys. One story involved the Greers, an "old pioneer" family in the Marvel area south and east of the park.

The old patriarch of the family had two daughters. The only way you had to get anywhere was to walk or hitchhike. One of the girls was milking, called her dad and told him there were some fellows walking up the road. The old man said to them, "you girls go into the house; we don't know who they are." One of the girls said to him it was just a couple of CCC boys from down at the camp. And he said to them, "Ok well take the cows in too."

Or at least that was how John McNamara remembered it!

Not all the CCCers' outside activities would have met with approval, from the army or any other New Dealer. McNamara reminisced, "Well, I can tell you where the bootlegger was between Mancos and Mesa Verde. The guys ... were older than I was, and every time we went by they had to stop and get a drink."

As the CCC days at Mesa Verde wound down, the young men who had worked there could be proud of their accomplishments. In honor of the fourth anniversary of the CCC, the March 31, 1937, *Cliff Dweller* listed some of their accomplishments over the previous three years. These included construction and maintenance of buildings, fences, walks, parking areas, and overlooks. They had also helped build water pipe and sewer lines and underground power and phone lines, run surveys, built 96 "table and bench combinations" and made "seed collections."

Add to that their efforts in a general cleanup, plus the projects previously mentioned, and the sweep of the CCC at Mesa Verde can be appreciated.

Writing about his experiences as a foreman, Robert Coates posed the question, "do the boys like the camp and the opportunity to work?" He felt very positive: "The best answer is found in the fact that approximately two-thirds of them have re-enlisted for the winter camp [1934-35], the rest having either returned to school or obtained work elsewhere."

Looking back over his Mesa Verde CCC days, Herb Hawkins spoke for many when he observed what it meant to him. "You could do what you wanted to do at the CCC. Learn all the trades....They did do a lot of good. You got all your medical, your food – and the food was good – and you got your place to live."

The young men found out that they had left a part of their lives behind when they left the CCC camp and returned to "civilian" life. "Take a kid my age, you learn about life very quickly," reflected John McNamara. "You find out you are not a kid any more. You are an adult and you act like an adult. You just grew up. After that I was on my own."

Jim Holston concurred and added another insight. "I was in trouble in school when I quit and went in. It gave me something to do and I settled down." After his CCC stint, he returned to high school and graduated. As for his experience he offered a somewhat contrary set of opinions with one definite conclusion, "I had a lot of fun, it was not hard work. There was a lot of hard work, but it was fun."

He also added a result that probably the designers of the New Deal had not anticipated. "A lot of kids came into the CCC and married a local girl and stayed there." A job during the depression, learning a skill or trade, finishing an education, a tour of duty in a national park, and wedding bells – the Civilian Conservation Corps offered "the opportunity of a lifetime."

"It was a growing up education," Coyne Thompson believed, summarizing what it meant to him.

> By the time you left, you were able to cope with the world at large. It was a good experience, there wasn't any doubt about it. And one thing about it was that everybody was in the same financial predicament and you didn't feel embarrassed because there wasn't anybody who was any other way.

The CCC remembrances of Mesa Verde provide an insight into an era. These young fellows, like their contemporaries in other camps, spent a "tour" or two, and in a few cases more, and then moved on with the rest of their lives. Mesa Verde National Park was richer for their having been there and, no doubt, in most cases they were as well.

Some of the boys probably reacted somewhat like Mark Twain's famous quote. "I love work. Why, sir, when I have a piece of work to perform, I go away to myself, sit down in the shade, and muse over the coming enjoyment. Sometimes I muse too long."

For the vast majority, nonetheless, the Civilian Conservation Corps experience did more for them than just provide a job and a place to live.

2

A GLIMPSE OF THE CCC AT MESA VERDE

Tree planting in 1935 after the disastrous Wetherill Mesa fire of the year before.

T he work projects at Mesa Verde seemed almost as varied as the backgrounds of the young men who labored to complete them. Actually their work proved to be not that much different from what their compatriots were doing elsewhere in parks, national forests, and throughout the country. All told, America and Americans benefited from the Civilian Conservation Corps.

To gain an idea of the magnitude of the effort, here is just some of the work accomplished between 1933 and 1942:

> More than two billion trees planted
> 13,100 miles of trails built
> More than six million man-days fighting forest fires
> 52,000 acres of public campground development
> 89,000 miles of telephone lines laid
> 3,400 fire lookout towers built

The CCCers at Mesa Verde, joining the other 57,000 who served in Colorado, played their role in all of these projects. As President Roosevelt had noted in his July 17, 1933, address, the young men of the CCC would do "work which is needed now and for the future and will bring a definite financial gain to the people of the nation."

The superintendent's driveway, at his home in the park, gets improved.

Laying an underground telephone cable at the park headquarters in 1937.

Painting the park equipment shed on a warm summer day.

Winter brought snow and cold but the CCCers kept working.

February 1936 found the boys trying to keep the main road open.

Preparing the footing for an equipment shed with the deep well's tower in the background.

The CCCers fashioned a variety of items for the park in their carpenter shop, which is now the bookstore.

Maintaining and working on the roads provided hours of "enjoyment."

Point Lookout looms in the background as CCCers clear rock and debris from yet another slide on the infamous Knife Edge Road.

Start of construction of the fire lookout station at Park Point in 1940.

A CCC curbing project well underway in the headquarters area of the park.

Leveling the land in preparation for finishing the tennis courts.

Getting ready to build new public campsites in April 1935.

3

WORKING FOR THE CCC
ON THE MESA VERDE

T he young men who joined the Civilian Conservation Corps came to Mesa Verde National Park to work on projects designed to improve the park, its facilities, and its accessibility to the broader public. The first CCC camp was established in 1933, in Prater Canyon just past the present-day campground and tunnel, on the park road leading to the mesa and the Far View ruins. It was located right beside the famed Knife Edge entrance into the park, where CCCers would spend many hours clearing and maintaining the road.

Residents of that first camp, NP-2-C, worked in the park during the summer and early fall of 1933. They constructed temporary lodging in the canyon and worked on conservation and camp projects during their stay. Company 861 became the first permanent camp in the park when it moved into the reconditioned Prater Canyon site on April 15, 1934. However, the Prater Canyon facility – a combination of tents and barracks – proved to be hot during the day and cold at night, so work would soon begin on a permanent camp for them near the park headquarters.

PRIORITIES SHIFTED DRAMATICALLY, THOUGH, ON JULY 9 WHEN THE GREAT MESA VERDE FIRE OF 1934 BROKE OUT. THE BLAZE WAS THE MOST SERIOUS FIRE IN THE PARK SINCE ITS CREATION IN 1906... .

With the creation of Company 861 in 1934, Lt. L.J. Lincoln, the army construction officer, and E.H. Lewiston, the civilian construction superintendent, arrived on April 10 to supervise the reconditioning of the Prater Canyon camp. The men of 861 and its supervisory personnel arrived several days later, including Camp Superintendent James W. Townsend, miscellaneous foreman Fred Trotter, and landscape foreman Lawrence Cone. The boys began work on April 17, two days after their arrival on the Rio Grande Southern Railroad from Nogales, Arizona.

During the spring and early summer of 1934, Company 861 worked on projects designed to improve the park prior to the arrival of the summer tourists. They rounded and sloped the shoulders of the roads between the information plaza and Spruce Tree plaza and on the new ruin road connection. They were assigned general cleanup, as the new ruin road uncovered old trash dumps which needed to be cleaned out. They also removed brush and logs along the gravel pit road, and cleaned up the area around the old utility area. The CCC boys also worked that summer on improving the

THREE CAMPS IN ALL

There would be a total of three CCC camps over the nine-year span of the CCC's presence in Mesa Verde. The first CCCers, a seasonal unit, had set up at NP-2-C in Prater Canyon in 1933, but left before winter. Then Company 861 reoccupied this site for awhile in 1934, before relocating to Camp NP-5-C and then to NP-6-C in the headquarters area. They remained in NP-6-C from fall 1934 until 1937. Company 1843 also was initially lodged at Prater Canyon (in the original NP-2-C camp), and then followed Company 861 into Camp NP-5-C (which was temporarily referred to as DNP-5-C because Company 1843 had originally been a Drought company). When Company 1843 was disbanded in 1937, it disappeared and its camp (NP-5-C) was allocated to Company 861, the surviving unit. At that time, NP-6-C was closed.

aesthetic appearance of the parking area and quarrying rock for curbing in the headquarters area. They inaugurated work on the new campground, removing trees and brush in preparation for the new campsites and roads. Whenever possible, trees and bushes from this area were transplanted to clearings or to road obliteration projects. Road obliteration became a major initiative as old roads in the headquarters area were eliminated and replanted. The CCC crews also worked on foot trails, filled old drainage ditches in the headquarters area, worked on cleaning pottery in the museum exhibits, began an insect control project to eliminate tent caterpillars that threatened vegetation on Chapin Mesa, and cleaned up wherever needed.

Work in the spring and summer of 1934 could be extremely tedious. Four men working in the museum exhibit area, for example, cleaned 3,786 potsherds with a weak hydrochloric acid solution. Ranger Chester Markley's crews harvested 45,168 tent caterpillar webs and burned them with kerosene. Markley praised the work of the men from Company 861, estimating that each man in his work group harvested about 200 "tents" per day. He claimed that was an increase of 78 tents per man per day over what the CCCers employed on this task in 1933 had accomplished. Their greater success, he said, was due to a heavier infestation resulting from a mild winter and early spring, as well as to the more "intelligent and enthusiastic" crew.

Priorities shifted dramatically, though, on July 9 when the great Mesa Verde fire of 1934 broke out. The blaze was the most serious fire in the park since its creation in 1906, and it raged for two weeks, until it was brought under control July 24. The CCC boys of Company 861 fought the park fire from beginning to end and were joined by additional volunteers from the Montezuma Valley and the New Mexico Indian reservations.

In the midst of the fire, the earliest enrollees of a second CCC unit, Company 1843, arrived at Mesa Verde on July 19. The next day, with the fire still raging out of control, 27 enrollees from the new company were transported to a temporary – or "fly" – camp on Wickiup Mesa, where they remained on fire patrol until July 24.

The disastrous 5,000-acre fire provided work for the young men who came to Mesa Verde for several years thereafter. For example, after the 1934 fire the enrollees spent considerable time and energy building fire roads and removing or pruning burned vegetation in the fire-damaged forest. Simultaneously, work began on a new campsite for the men from Company 861 that would eliminate the 11-mile commute from Prater Canyon to the park headquarters.

In 1934, as the men of Company 1843 arrived between July 19 and August 9, the company assumed control of the Prater Canyon site, and Company 861 moved to its new camp in the headquarters area. At last, its enrollees believed, they had found a permanent home; but soon the park received approval for two winter camps, which necessitated the construction of another permanent camp to which Company 861 would move after its brief stay in NP-5-C. Meanwhile the CCCers returned to the tasks that occupied them prior to the fire. Four men continued to work in the museum repairing pottery, filling out catalog cards, restoring designs on repaired pottery and sketching the pottery in black and white and color. Park Superintendent Ernest P. Leavitt commended the artistic work of J.G. Allen, in particular, for his part in sketching the artifacts.

Company 1843 eventually reached its full strength of 211 men on August 9. The army personnel in the company were Capt. Leo A. Noble, camp commander; Lt. F.W. Thomas, Jr., personnel officer; and Lt. Col. E. J. Condit, camp surgeon. The Technical Services supervisory and facilitating personnel were Jeremiah J. "Pop" Drennan, project superintendent; Floyd L. Boardman, engineering foreman; George R. McCormack, forestry foreman; Kenneth M. Saunders, landscape foreman; and Timothy Jones, mechanic. The new enrollees first had to complete their orientation to CCC and receive their physicals and inoculations before they could begin work. Even with those tasks completed, CCCers in Company 1843 were unable to begin offsite work because their leaders, equipment, and clothing were slow to arrive. Those who were able to work began on the obliteration of a section of the old road within walking distance of the Prater Canyon camp.

Gradually, the equipment and leaders arrived, and perhaps most importantly, the trucks. A Dodge stake truck transferred from Company 861, four new GMC stake body trucks and two dump trucks reached the Prater Canyon site by August 19. One of the first projects was to fit the stake trucks with seats so CCCers could be transported to their tasks. As the men worked on improving the road, the supervisors built a small section as a model to provide the inexperienced men with a vision of what they

RED TAPE AND THE CCC

The CCC was a vast federal bureaucracy that attempted to coordinate the efforts of four separate departments (Army, Agriculture, Interior, and Labor), each of which had its own record-keeping procedures. Robert Fechner and three assistants headed the ECW leadership, which reported directly to President Roosevelt and worked closely with the four department secretaries. Each camp commander, project supervisor and local technical agency superintendent had monthly reporting responsibilities.

For young CCCer Robert Beers, preparing those reports was both boring and infuriating because it kept him in the office. He had to type monthly and summary reports that detailed the activities of his friends, while they were outside "shooting porcupine" or working on construction projects in the park. His position entitled him to a cold lunch, but denied him the friendly banter of lunch with fellow CCCers around picnic tables at the remote hot kitchens.

The surviving reports for Mesa Verde describe projects undertaken, man-days of work completed, brief descriptions of the jobs being done, and all expenditures for non-CCCer costs such as equipment, maintenance, supplies, miscellaneous expenses and skilled labor. Other enrollees describe similar reports for the Army detailing absences, illnesses, medication, and injuries. Most of this massive "paper trail" reached the National Archives during or after World War II, but has never been organized or processed.

sought to accomplish. With their transportation problems solved, a new road foreman named Eaton and 25 men began sloping the banks of the main highway adjacent to Prater Canyon while another foreman, Quinn, and nine men began building curbing on the main highway near the headquarters. Because this work was done at a great distance from the Prater Canyon camp, Superintendent Townsend of Company 861 supervised the work on the curbing project. A final project was initiated in Morefield Canyon, where an earthen dam and spillway were built to improve runoff control and provide a water containment facility. With as many as 40 CCCers involved in this project, it was the largest undertaken by Company 1843 in the late summer and fall of 1934.

Project Superintendent Drennan reported to E.P. Leavitt that 23 boys were constantly engaged in camp overhead and operation each month. In his report of October 1, 1934, Drennan wrote that the long trip from the Prater Canyon camp to headquarters or down to Mancos necessitated careful planning of transportation so that the trucks hauled men and materials to headquarters and returned with supplies and wood for the army. The weather had been moderate, he noted, but September had permitted only 19 work days as there were five weekends and the Labor Day holiday.

The major projects continued to be the bank sloping – which included boulder removal and cribbing along the road to minimize the dangers of their rolling onto the main road below – and the building of the ponds for fish and game in Morefield Canyon. Other activities included moving a gas tank to the new permanent fuel storage area, draining and refilling the radiators nightly, sharpening and repairing tools, and even installing a bulletin board outside the camp office. The work of the enrollees had been little affected by illness and there had been no injuries.

In his November report to Superintendent Leavitt, Drennan noted that on October 10 Company 1843 finally moved from Prater Canyon into its new camp near park headquarters. Drennan wrote that the transfer from Prater Canyon had been accomplished with "[b]ut slight interruption to work on projects."

> The men were taken to work at the usual hour after breakfasts. Our trucks were then lent to the army who paid for the extra gas consumed by our trucks in moving them. Lunch was served on the job. The gangs were then brought back to the old camp a little earlier than usual so that the men could load property for which they were responsible and were moved to new camp in time for supper.

This operation illustrated the varied and separate responsibilities at Mesa Verde. The U.S. Army had responsibility for the camp life of the enrollees, and the Technical Services and project superintendents, such as Drennan, oversaw the workday activities of the CCCers in their approved projects. Drennan noted the coordination in his report.

> This change in base of our operations necessitated adjustments usual to new conditions and presented new problems, the satisfactory solution of which required cooperation between the technical service and the army.

When Company 1843 moved to South Chapin Mesa in October, the army was responsible for obliterating the remnants of the first camp, and Drennan reported that the bank sloping operations provided suitable fill for the latrines and pits that the army needed to remediate. The enrollees also helped the army construct the fresh fruit and vegetable cellar at the new camp DNP-5-C, helped with a parking area in the camp, and did other work to landscape and improve the area.

While a small number of the enrollees worked on these projects, the majority continued with the bank sloping near Knife Edge, which involved "21,000 square yards of work" along the highway. Drennan described the project.

Most of this was on high banks which had developed sags. The overhanging edge was cut away, loose boulders removed and base pillowed. Shallow banks have been sloped and planted to conform with ideas of park landscape engineers.

He also reported that two slabs of sandstone at Knife Edge were being drilled and demolished, with the larger pieces removed to headquarters for use in the parking area wall.

Other activities included installing high altitude jets in a Ford V-8 pick-up truck, and similar adjustment to one of the GMC trucks. Both actions were taken in an effort to reduce fuel consumption and hence project cost. He also reported that he had requested hoops and canvas covers for the trucks so the men could be safely transported in the impending winter weather.

James Townsend made similar reports on the activities of Company 861. He noted that as Company 1843 moved into Camp NP-5-C on South Chapin Mesa, Company 861 moved into its new facilities at NP-6-C on North Chapin Mesa. Both of these moves had resulted from the administrative approval that granted Mesa Verde National Park two winter camps. For the next three years, Mesa Verde had two permanent camps, until the two companies were combined, and 861 was moved to 1843's camp.

In his October 1934 report Townsend noted that the men of Company 861 had repaired the roof of the park administration building; worked 462 man days constructing 1,800 feet of 4-foot paths in the vicinity of Camp NP-6-C; cleared building sites for the erection of housekeeping cabins for seasonal employees; completed construction of the engineering office building; worked on relocating the government mess hall, cooler, bunkhouse and coalhouse; formulated plans and surveys for CCC work of both camps; transplanted 345 plants to beautify the landscape of both the camps and the park headquarters; quarried and shaped rock used in and around the camps; and continued to repair the museum exhibits under the supervision of Park Naturalist Paul R. Franke. Superintendent Townsend concluded his October report by explaining that the relocation of the enrollees in their new quarters had prompted "a great improvement in morale."

In November Townsend reported that company strength had increased from 161 to 184, with approximately 35 men detailed to the camp work, ill or absent. This meant that the field work force for the CCC projects was approximately 80 percent of the total manpower in Company 861. Townsend reported that 30 LEMs (Local Experienced Men) had arrived on November 10 via transfer from CCC Camp F-28-C, Beaver Camp near Dolores, Colorado. Good weather had prevailed at Mesa Verde until November 16, when the camp received rain, sleet and finally snow, he

MAN DAYS

In November and December of 1934, Superintendent Drennan described the work done on the active projects and now added the number of "man-days" (abbreviated here as MD) expended on each project. (Outside work depended upon sun time, but men never left before 7 a.m. and returned by 4:30 p.m., so a man day likely averaged between seven and eight hours.)

PROJECT #	TYPE OF PROJECT	# OF MAN DAYS
1	telephone lines	65 MD
11	general cleanup	70 MD
14B	foot trails	266 MD
16	maintenance of dwellings	173 MD
17	housekeeping cabins	811 MD
28	2 sheds for motor equipment	734 MD
30	fence range	895 MD
44	a linear survey	108 MD
46C	erosion control	2073 MD
53A	old road obliteration	63 MD
53E	planting obliterated road	46 MD
56C	guardrail and quarry operation for curbing	167 MD
57	pumping water from deep well	12 MD
no project #	removal of fire hazards	151 MD

noted. Between November 16 and 30, approximately 10 inches of snow had fallen, but it never exceeded two inches per day and it always melted quickly and so did not impair the work. In addition to continuing several of the projects he described the previous month, he listed several new ones: stringing wire for a new three-circuit telephone system; construction of minor roads in the campground; preparation for snow removal on roads and highways; acquisition of logs for construction of garages and repair of roofs for permanent dwellings at the park headquarters; removal of insect-infested trees on Chapin Mesa; and landscaping work on the headquarters parking area. He also reported the arrival of equipment: trucks, a Caterpillar tractor, and long-handled shovels.

As is evident from Townsend's lists of fall 1934 activities, the oversight and accounting for these specific projects and the appropriation of funds for their completion occupied both the CCC superintendents, who bore a heavy load of responsibility for administrative coordination. Reflective of the delicate balancing necessary to complete the CCC projects was a November 16, 1934, letter to Townsend from K.M. Saunders, superintendent of construction. Saunders explained that because actual expenditures of $1,510 exceeded the amount allocated for the construction of the bunkhouse, there was no money to hire a plasterer to finish the project; consequently, he asked Townsend to find CCC boys who could complete the project with the materials on hand. Estimated and actual costs had exceeded the allocation by 28 cents and included the following supplies: lumber, shingles, nails, sash, wiring materials, light fixtures, paint and floor finish, cement and sand, equipment, overhead, plastering supplies, and miscellaneous. Such fiscal accountability issues plagued the local superintendents, technical agencies, and the CCC projects throughout their history in Mesa Verde, and likely throughout the entire CCC program.

Superintendent Drennan reported in 1934 that the camp numbered 190 enrollees and 15 facilitating personnel in November and 149 enrollees and 32 LEMs in December. He also asked Superintendent Leavitt on December 13 to add four special projects to the camp project inventory. Aimed at strengthening morale and simultaneously improving camp life during the winter months, he suggested building a fireplace in the recreation hall and reading and writing rooms in each of the five barracks, building winter sports facilities (a toboggan and ski course, ice rink, and handball court), enlarging the garage to accommodate two passenger cars, and creating convenient parking facilities for the camp. Drennan claimed that these amenities, coupled with improvements such as the camp flagpole, bachelor quarters for supervisory personnel, and the root cellar, had improved the camp facilities and personnel conditions.

Though he did not propose the special projects that Drennan identified, James Townsend made a similar report for December. Company 861 had 184 men in camp at the beginning of the month and 180 on December 28. Almost half their time was spent on two projects, dwellings for seasonal and temporary staff and planting trees and shrubs. The much despised insect control work took nearly 200 man-days, more than road work and snow removal combined. One hundred man-days were spent on museum exhibit repair. Townsend welcomed the arrival, on December 6, of First Lt. J.H. Gray, to assume the duties of camp doctor for Company 861. (Up to that point, Col. Condit of Company 1843 had served as the doctor for both companies.) The careful description of progress and costs attached to CCC projects did not include the cost of enrollee (Emergency Conservation Work) labor This expense was carried only as man-days worked and was not otherwise calculated in the expenditures. The national authorization of positions for CCCers constituted the commitment for their wages and attendant expenses such as government-issue clothing, food, shelter, and such. For practical purposes the CCCers cost the taxpayers, but not the federal agencies for which they worked.

January posed unique opportunities and challenges for the CCCers working on the Mesa Verde. In his January 1935 report, Project Superintendent Townsend explained that a severe snowstorm beginning on

January 10 and concluding on January 20 generated a total snowfall of 17 inches with approximately 10 inches on the ground at any time during this 10-day period. While no time had been lost in Company 861, the actual progress on projects was slowed by the winter weather. All dirt roads had become muddy, some nearly impassable; the conditions endangered all of the mechanical equipment which became clogged with mud. Townsend explained that the tractors used on the roads were especially vulnerable because their track rollers had to be cleaned out at the end of each day lest they freeze up during the cold evenings.

On the other hand, the bad weather permitted the assignment of nine men to Park Naturalist Franke's museum exhibit repair. Among other projects the enrollees assisted with construction of the much admired Mesa Verde dioramas. Starting with the miniature of Step House Cave, the CCC team worked through the winter of 1935.

"WE FIND THAT BY TAKING AN INTEREST IN THEM AND SHOWING APPRECIATION FOR THEIR EFFORTS, THE MEN RESPOND WITH MORE AND BETTER WORK."

Meanwhile, J.J. Drennan described the winter tribulations in Company 1843, which was unable to get their trucks started promptly on Monday, January 21; consequently all work began late that morning. Thereafter, Drennan assigned one of his truck drivers to run the truck engines intermittently throughout the night. The procedure proved successful and the ECW office recommended the same procedure for Company 861. Drennan also reported that effort and morale in Company 1843 had been improved by giving more attention to the enrollees and their problems. He concluded, "We find that by taking an interest in them and showing appreciation for their efforts, the men respond with more and better work."

February 1935 witnessed continued bad weather. Superintendent Townsend reported a monthly snowfall of 35 inches with 10 inches on February 13 and 15 inches during the night of February 14. The camp doctor recommended that the men be released from work during the February 13 snowstorm, but Townsend noted that the work was made up on Saturday, thus averting time lost for the month of February. The museum exhibits were progressing rapidly with two exhibits cleaned, repaired, and returned to their cases. Additionally, work on the miniature model of Step House Cave had gone quickly, and was nearly finished. With the cave itself completed, the unfinished work consisted of adding the shrubbery and wax figures of the inhabitants.

During the same month Drennan explained that Company 1843 had spent 881 man-days maintaining the side roads used by the CCCers to haul men and supplies. The tractors occasionally had to be used to pull trucks out of the mud. On several occasions the roads were closed and the supplies were pulled into work areas by tractor-drawn sleds.

Conditions improved in spring 1935, which allowed the CCCers to begin work on a broader range of outdoor projects. Because Companies 861 and 1843 had earned the designation "winter camps," Park Superintendent Leavitt had requested a broad range of projects for the fall and winter of 1934-35 so that the men "could be employed to advantage throughout this period." Associate ECW Director A.E. Demaray questioned Leavitt as to why only 22 percent of the 36 projects started at the park had been completed, and 41 percent were less than 25 percent completed. Leavitt explained in a May 22 memorandum that he had felt it necessary to seek approval for many projects so that "when weather conditions prevented work on one project, there were other projects available to which the men could be assigned." Demaray encouraged Leavitt to complete these unfinished projects within the fifth enrollment period.

...TOWNSEND'S REPORT INDICATED THAT COMPANY 861 ...HAD MORE WORK RELATED TO WILDLIFE AND THE NATURAL SETTINGS OF THE PARK: SEEDING, MOVING TREES AND SHRUBS, AND PLANTING IN THE FIELD; WILDLIFE RECONNAISSANCE; AND TEMPORARY CHECK-DAMS.

As Companies 861 and 1843 entered the fifth enrollment period which began on April 1, 1935, the park service requested new projects to occupy the men in the companies. In Townsend's report for April 1935, he noted that the enrollees had spent 2,529 man-days on a combination of projects which included the construction of dwellings and garages, pipe and tile lines, sign markers and monuments, minor roads, and a new contact station. In addition, the CCCers performed highway maintenance, field planting or seeding, insect control, moving and planting trees, lineal surveys, and topographical surveys. Superintendent Drennan reported the next month that Company 1843 had logged 3,892 man-days, half again as many as what Townsend had reported for Company 861 the previous month. Such a great difference could have been due to the number of men in the company, but also to the number of work days in the month and the effect of weather on outside projects. Their work included building maintenance and improvements, infrastructure improvements (telephone, water supply, and fences), road work, landscaping, transportation of materials and surveys.

Company 1843 had 225 men on May 1 and 219 on May 31. Throughout the month the company commander held approximately 35 men for camp activities such as food preparation and service, camp cleanup, secretarial duties, motor pool, and such. An average of 176 CCCers did fieldwork during the month. The company rolls included 19 LEMs, 10 technical or army leaders, and 18 enrollees serving as assistant leaders.

During the same month Superintendent Townsend's report indicated that Company 861 undertook some projects similar to those done by 1843, but had more work related to wildlife and the natural settings of the park: seeding, moving trees and shrubs, and planting in the field; wildlife reconnaissance; and temporary check-dams. By late spring 1935 both companies were participating in a number of common work projects such as dwelling construction and maintenance, construction of garages, landscaping, and surveys. Though the individual companies had their own projects, Company 861 seemed to have a broader range of projects than Company 1843, a concern that J.J. Drennan had raised on several occasions. Townsend acknowledged this same disparity in his August 1935 report, noting, "The great difference in the amount of orders between the camps was mainly due to NP-6-C [Company 861] having 24 projects under way during the month and NP-5-C [Company 1843] only had 11."

In August 1935 the men in Company 861 started to work on the cabinets and furniture in the park museum. Beginning first on the cabinets, and expanding in September to chairs, they carved them so as to be consistent with other museum furniture, making them of pine with leather seats. By the end of the year, they had completed 10 chairs and two cabinets. They also began construction of picnic tables for the new public campground. They revisited the check-dams they had constructed on Wetherill Mesa to minimize erosion from the fire-burned area. When a three-day rain filled all of the dams to capacity, the enrollees returned to raise the height of the dams and, thus, better control erosion.

On September 30, 1935, the fifth enrollment period ended and Superintendent Townsend praised the completion of the public campground on which both companies had worked. The new campground, located behind or just north of the park service complex by Spruce Tree House, more than doubled the capacity of its predecessor. It included new campsites, picnic tables for both day- and overnight-visitors, and a new campfire circle due north of the superintendent's home. This campground is still in use for daytime picnicking near the park headquarters and museum. J.J. Drennan reported that Company 1843 had also completed three

A stone hogan built by the CCC.

projects by the end of the fifth period: the contact station, the campground fireplaces and the campground fuel and water stations. Drennan reported that the water stations – cedar post drinking fountains – had originally been assigned to 861, but had been completed by 1843 to balance work-loads after the picnic tables were transferred to 861. He also noted that Harry A. Phillips, an educational adviser, arrived on September 10, 1935, the first person in that capacity for Company 1843.

During the fall of 1935 the two companies spent the majority of their time working on five housekeeping cabins and two Indian hogans used by Navajos on the staff. The work included both construction of the dwellings by Company 861 and the provision of water and sewage connections by Company 1843. Work continued through the winter, and the housekeeping and hogan dwellings were nearly complete by late spring 1936.

In his report for March 1936, James Townsend noted a temporary crisis in morale that followed an announcement on March 18 that Company 861 was to be discontinued on April 1. Within a week, however, it was reinstated for the seventh enrollment period (April 1-September 30, 1936). In September 1936, Company 861's strength had fallen from 122 men at the beginning of the month to a mere 86 at its close. Townsend attributed this drop to the close of the sixth enrollment period and the decisions of

NAVAJO HISTORY IN MESA VERDE

It is impossible to know when the first Navajo people entered Mesa Verde. Early pictures of C.B. Kelley at his Spruce Tree cabin appear to have native people there. In 1921 when Superintendent Jesse Nusbaum outlined his program for Mesa Verde, it provided for building four Navajo hogans. Nusbaum had worked with Native American people in New Mexico before coming to Mesa Verde and understood their cultural needs.

Courtesy William C. Winkler/Ansel Hall

Early Navajo hogans at Mesa Verde.

Ansel F. Hall was the National Park Service chief of education (now called interpretation), and as such was responsible for the creation of museums in the national parks. Nusbaum, in fact, reported to him on the Mesa Verde Museum, and the two worked together to achieve the museum visitors enjoy today. Hall had been successful in obtaining Rockefeller family donations for the Yosemite Museum and introduced the family to Nusbaum and Mesa Verde. Years later, as the owner of the Mesa Verde Company, Hall would employ Navajo workers in his tourist services within the park.

When the Civilian Conservation Corps became active in Mesa Verde, they replaced the original traditional wood and mud Navajo hogans with eight substantial cut-stone structures in keeping with the other park residences. These served the Navajo staff very well over the years and allowed them to live in harmony with their cultural values. As the staff grew it was necessary to add canvas units to serve some members of the seasonal staff. A central utility building provided toilets, lavatories, showers and laundry facilities.

Sam Yellowhorse and Sandoval Begaye became the social leaders of Navajo workers in the park. They all worked well together and provided a steady work force for the National Park Service and the Mesa Verde Company. Several Navajos retired from the park service after 30-plus years of service and two Mesa Verde Company employees had more than 25 years of service. We always had a seasonal weaver and silversmith on hand to explain their crafts to the public. The Navajos' evening songs and dances at campfire circle were the "frosting on the cake."

– William C. Winkler

(William C. Winkler worked with the Mesa Verde Company for many years, starting as a seasonal employee and eventually running the company. Ansel Hall was his father-in-law.)

ENROLLMENT DECREASES

Company strength fluctuated as the eighth enrollment period ended. With the national economy beginning a slow recovery, some CCCers found jobs; others became disillusioned with life in the camps or seriously homesick. As national conditions slowly improved, the importance of the stipend to family members at home declined in importance as a retention tool. Leaving the CCC, whether through resignation or simply walking away (going AWOL) had few consequences except that CCCers might not be able to reenroll in the CCC.

many men not to reenlist for the seventh period. Company 1843 experienced similar difficulties in retaining its enrollee complement. While there had been approximately 146 men in July, the company size had fallen to 89 by the end of October. Still, they continued to maintain two separate companies, each with its own camp and staff until 1937.

The ninth enrollment period (April 1-September 30, 1937) work projects in Mesa Verde bear remarkable similarity to those approved during 1934-35 because the guidelines for CCC initiatives remained consistent over time. Newly recruited CCCers continued to turn their attention to road work, wildlife and habitat projects, landscaping, reforestation, building maintenance, weed control and trail work, infrastructure improvements (water, sewer, corrals, lighting), and fire lookouts. For the remaining years until its dissolution in 1942 the CCCers at Mesa Verde would continue to perform the same types of work. The only significant change in their lives came after war began in Europe in 1939. By 1940, CCCers received fieldwork credit for up to eight hours of general defense training in practical or vocational courses such as shop mathematics, cooking, road construction, and first aid as well as eight hours of basic training in hygiene, mathematics, and English. Later CCCers remembered that this training helped their transition into the armed forces once the United States entered World War II after the Pearl Harbor attack.

4

"A Lot of Fun Doing It:" the Dioramas

From left: Meredith Guillet, Paul Franke and Kenny Ross planning a diorama, November 1934.

O ne of the most popular Mesa Verde exhibits, since the day they arrived on the scene, has been the museum dioramas. Without question, they have achieved what the park service hoped they would. A 1939 report summarized that goal. The dioramas "will enable thousands of park visitors to visualize ancient life and people as they existed in those early days and thus be able to view the ruins with better understanding and greater appreciation."

The Civilian Conservation Corps assisted in creating four of the five dioramas visitors see today in the Mesa Verde Museum. A diorama is a three-dimensional scene in miniature, depicting a setting with plants, animals, people and structures as if frozen in time. The first, depicting Folsom Man, was made in Berkeley, California, at the Western Museum Laboratories of the National Park Service. Placed in the park museum in the spring of 1937, it appeared after the next two in the series chronologically (Basket Makers and modified Basket Makers) were already finished and on display. The White Dog site in Arizona served as the model for the Basket Maker diorama. The Developmental Pueblo exhibit (a composite of the Far View site) then followed. The last one, constructed in the winter of 1937-38, featured the Great or Classic Pueblo period and dramatized a day at Spruce Tree House.

The goal of this project was simply, "to make a comprehensive exhibit that the public would understand." All of the dioramas helped to catch viewers' attention and make history come alive for young and old alike.

Construction of each diorama followed a common sequence. A site was chosen, for example the Step House Cave with its modified Basket Maker Village. Then a "penciled study" was produced "based on photographs and actual measurements."

The next pivotal step focused on constructing a small working model. This provided a test "of the work's feasibility and a model by which to make the large habitat group, as it would be much easier to make corrections to the small model." After the work proved feasible and the "bugs" had been worked out, construction started on the frame for the larger model.

Then followed the background, shrubs, trees, and any structures (in the case of Step House there were two Basket Maker houses). Human figures (finely modeled of wax), baskets, weapons, ornaments, and other "items" completed the task of producing a "habitat group." The instructors were so determined to provide authenticity that CCCers made tiny pots, painted them with authentic designs, and then broke them to create tiny potsherds, which they scattered on the "ground." The finished exhibit would be about four feet by five feet, with a depth of four feet.

When completed, the set illustrated five important periods of southwestern and Mesa Verde settlement. Each captured the people "in attitudes of daily task processes."

The July 1933 issue of "Mesa Verde Notes" described the Step House diorama.

> The scene reproduced is during the time of harvest and storage for winter. The women are busy with the corn, one bringing in the husked ears in a basket, another placing it in a storage cyst [sic], a child mends a basket, a mother grinding the corn to meal with metate and mano, an old man bringing in fagots.

Hidden artificial light illuminated the scene.

The work took time and dedication to complete. For instance, eight CCC men worked on the Step House diorama at one time or another, contributing more than 1,100 man-days.

Kenneth Ross and Meredith Guillet (later Mesa Verde superintendent) were singled out for special praise, but CCCers worked on the diorama, as well. The narrative report on the project praised them highly, noting they did work of the "highest quality."

> They have developed a real interest in their work and their spirit is to be commended and it also, in every way, reflects a credit to their instructors, Park Naturalist Paul Franke and Ranger-

Historian Don Watson.

Artist and diorama expert Alfred Rowell, a Works Progress Administration artist, also deserves praise for his work in painting the scenery, refurbishing existing dioramas, and other contributions during his four-year stay at the park.

Various people, including Rowell, Kenny Ross, and the CCCers, are given credit for introducing touches of humor into the dioramas. Look carefully at the right side of the Spruce Tree House diorama. There stands a five-inch native scratching his head in disbelief, as he looks at "a kiva beam he had just chopped a foot too short with his stone axe." Visitors who study the dioramas carefully will notice other humorous touches as well.

Ross, who worked on three of the dioramas, described what went into constructing them. Hired as a Local Experienced Man, Ross worked with the CCC. He, the CCCers (the "boys were picked carefully for the project") and others had "a lot of fun doing it."

> We started the morning with a cup of coffee when we got in our tiny workroom. We would talk over what went wrong yesterday and what were the plans for today. Meredith Guillet had natural talent in painting, my talents were pretty general – a knowledge of the archaeology of the area and the ability to work with my hands. I experimented a lot and made a lot of stuff that had to be thrown away. It was largely experimental; we had little to go by.
>
> The figures are all built of beeswax and Peruvian fir balsam. One of the problems was to make things look natural in miniature form.
>
> In no case did we use native rock; it would not fit the scale. The rock is all plaster of Paris or a mixture of plaster of Paris and papier-mâché. We did use wood being careful that the grain faced inward or disguising it. I did the pottery, all of it out of plaster of Paris. The baskets are molded from papier-mâché.

Watson, in a report, summarized the goal of the Step House Cave diorama, "All of the objects reproduced have been found during excavation of Late Basket Maker sites and every effort has been made to picture faithfully the lives of these people." The care taken to achieve this goal has pleased and fascinated generations of visitors.

Visitors to the national park in 1939 were the first to see all five dioramas telling the whole story of pre-historic occupation of the region. Wrote one, "I have worked on models and dioramas and know the possibilities and perils. I have visited most of the large museums all over the globe. But for downright good stuff loaded with human interest, I feel that you have trump cards in your five small cases."

Kenneth Ross and Meredith Guillet build the framework for the Step House diorama.

By January 1935, Ross and Guillet have made significant progress on the alcove setting for the diorama. Ross continued working at Mesa Verde after his CCC days there, and Guillet came back as park superintendent 30 years later.

By March 1935, after hundreds of hours of work, what had been only an idea is nearly completed.

With wax figures and other details now in place, the finished Step House diorama is finally ready for public viewing.

Kenneth Ross reproduced actual Mesa Verde pottery in miniature, using plaster of Paris and draftsman's ink. These are used in the Spruce Tree House diorama. Several such tiny vessels were decorated, then broken to depict potsherds.

Alfred Lee Rowell made the human figures in wax, Kenneth Ross the pottery. Items were made on a scale of ¾-inch to one foot, with some exaggeration of details for visual effect.

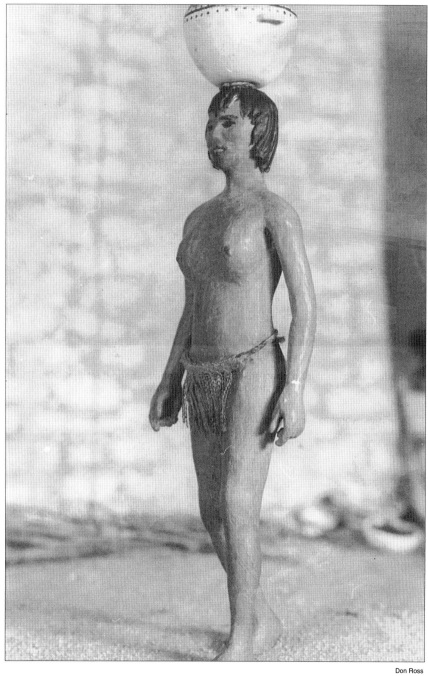

Don Ross

Human figures seem to come alive as they go about their daily life in the Spruce Tree House diorama.

**In the finished Spruce Tree House diorama, details in the figures,
artifacts and architecture depict the daily lives of villagers.**

By the spring of 1938, the Spruce Tree House diorama is ready for installation, helping park visitors envision life in the alcove.

5

LIFE IN THE MESA VERDE'S CCC CAMPS

C CC enrollees faced the distinctive challenges of isolation and homesickness when they arrived at almost any CCC camp. The reasons for the problems were numerous. The men were young, 18 to 25 when they enrolled, and some joined at an even younger age because $25 of their $30 per month wages was sent to their families.

The majority of the enrollees sent to Mesa Verde came from Colorado, New Mexico, Oklahoma, Texas, and occasionally Wyoming. The park's location in the remote Four Corners region of southwestern Colorado and its own remoteness from the Durango-Mancos-Cortez road created a truly isolated outpost. Even the few enrollees who came from the surrounding area had not likely visited the park, which would have been a day's travel – sometimes on foot – from nearby communities.

FOR THOSE COMING FROM URBAN AREAS LIKE CHEYENNE,
DENVER, OKLAHOMA CITY, OR FT. WORTH,
LIFE AT MESA VERDE WAS SHOCKING.

One of the rationales for the CCC had been to reaffirm America's attachment to the agrarian myth, which valued time in the countryside, where people were uncorrupted by urban life and benefited from clean air and hard, but "purifying" labor on the land. But the Mesa Verde enrollees often came from small rural communities. For those coming from urban areas like Cheyenne, Denver, Oklahoma City, or Ft. Worth, life at Mesa Verde was shocking. They often arrived without friends, with few belongings except the clothes on their backs, and suddenly found themselves in camps administered by military officers, normally army reserve officers. Arthur "Runt" Wilson, an enrollee whose family lived in the rural farming region north of Cortez, remembered that he occasionally walked home on weekends – a very long walk each way.

The camps themselves were modeled upon military camps in their construction and organization. The Mesa Verde buildings were wooden frame structures and were prototypical army barracks. When the camps were fully staffed the barracks each accommodated approximately 30 men, who slept army style on cots or bunks with footlockers placed near their beds. Upon arrival at Mesa Verde the men received a physical examination and were issued surplus army uniforms, or later the distinctive CCC uniforms. A *Kiva Krier* cartoon of October 4, 1935, satirized the distribution of the new uniforms, with the quartermaster inquiring of enrollees standing in line, "How do you want your uniforms. . . . too large or too small?" Once

CCC
NEWSPAPERS

The CCCers were encouraged to publish company newspapers, which interested volunteers created in their leisure hours. There is no evidence that the first temporary company in Prater Canyon had a newspaper, but both companies 861 and 1843, had newspapers by fall 1935 – the earliest surviving issues. Company 861's paper was the *Kiva Krier*, and 1843's was the *Mesa Verdian*. The two were similar in that each had an editor, an assistant editor, a cartoonist, several other CCCers and an adviser who was either one of the camp officers or the educational consultant assigned to the camp. The early papers were mimeographed, and looked much like high school newspapers of the time. The camp commander usually had a column and the staff reported on social activities (athletic contests, movies, dances, special celebrations and the comings and goings of the enrollees and their officers) for the CCCers. They often included a gossip column, safety or health columns prepared by the medical officers, and efforts at camp humor or satire that were normally unsigned.

On December 25, 1935, the first issue of the *Cliff Dweller*, a new joint publication of Companies 861 and 1843, was produced. Co-editors of the first issue were Platt Cline and Clarence Phillips, and Kenneth Ross and Percy Pino were its associate editors. The *Cliff Dweller* continued as a joint project until February 22, 1937, when it announced its "new policy" and became the exclusive newspaper of Company 861. By 1937 Kenneth Ross had become the editor; his associate was Harlan Elsten and his reporters were Geoff Hensley, Ed Parker and "Sinister Shadow." The printers and compositors were Ernest Widmar and John Lobato. The *Cliff Dweller* was printed on a press and had a professional appearance, but the basic structure remained the same – announcements, an editorial, an advice column, camp humor and satire, gossip about the CCCers, and personal information from former CCCers.

the enrollees got their work uniforms, they ordinarily spent several days, perhaps as long as a week, getting adjusted to the camp routine. In those early days the men were fed, taught about camp policies and procedures, and given instruction on the work regime that they would soon assume.

Consistent with the national policies of the Emergency Conservation Work Act and later the CCC, enrollees were carefully weighed and their health assessed. During its nine-year history the Civilian Conservation Corps collected a wealth of information about the young men who served in its camps. In order to ascertain how the CCC experience affected the enrollees, the military officers and camp surgeons made careful notes about the men. They examined and measured them, checked them for venereal diseases, and periodically brought dental teams to the camps so that the annual reports of the CCC could discuss how the experience had transformed young men who initially arrived as part of the New Deal relief effort.

The military officers understood that their responsibilities with the CCC included the transformation of often desperate, normally undernourished, and frequently illiterate enrollees into useful citizens. The task began immediately, but once the enrollees came under the daytime supervision of the park service personnel, military ambitions awaited evenings and weekends. No recordings exist of the initial remarks of the camp commanders, but in the October 18, 1935, issue of Company 861's *Kiva Krier*, Lt. Bertram E. Sandham, second in command, told CCCers that as in civilian life, they must obey the rules and regulations of the Civilian Conservation Corps, the law "by which you eat, live, work, learn and indulge in recreation." He explained that the military officers were the representatives of the CCC, which provided "food, shelter, beds, bedding, laundering, medical care, educational courses and athletics, in addition to the money which it pays you for your work."

He further explained that the enrollees "maintained clean and orderly barracks and beds, practiced bodily hygiene, and conducted themselves in the mess hall and elsewhere in keeping with the habits of a well-bred person." Both at work and in the camp the men were to obey the orders and advice of the foremen and officers. So long as the enrollees fulfilled their responsibilities, their lives in camp and on the job would be happy and provide fond memories, but insubordination could provoke punishment and even administrative discharge, which severed a man's relationship with the CCC and prevented future reenrollment.

In those first days in camp the enrollees learned about personal hygiene, and were introduced to the layout of the camps. In all likelihood the men also spent some time cleaning the toilets and showers, and doing a bit of "KP." As with most military operations, such tasks were usually reserved for individuals in need of discipline, but new enrollees also received an initial introduction to these tasks, perhaps to alert them to the potential con-

A MOTHER'S CONCERN

Lee Rice exemplifies the problems caused by separation from home and family. His mother Etta Rice of Henryetta, Oklahoma, wrote to President Roosevelt on April 30, 1937, advising him of her son's problems in adjusting to Company 861 at Mesa Verde. In an undated letter to her, young Lee described his misery.

> i had two chills last night and I have two sore arms[.] one I can't hardly lift where they shot me[.] my vacanition is taking[.] I espect it to have a scar about the size of a dime[.] it sure is sore[.] We went on a sit down strike yesterday because we wasn't getting enough too eat[.] it didn't come out so good. they won't give any one a transfer from this dam place because they can't hardly get anyone to come here. . . if I can't get a transfer I am coming out of here soon any ways[.] half-starving, bed bugery place my eyes are longing to see okla again and home sweet home.

Etta Rice wrote that she had sent five letters to her son, yet he had not received a single one of them. She claimed to have sent two more to the lieutenant but had not heard from him either. Unable to figure out to whom she should complain, she wrote to President Roosevelt. Though she initially feared that Lee was homesick, she claimed that her son was apparently "half starved," and asked the president to look into his situation as soon as possible. On June 11, 1937, Charles H. Taylor reported on the investigation of her son's situation at Mesa Verde. He explained in his report that an officer interviewed Lee, who now said that he was getting plenty of food, which was prepared properly. Lee also had overcome his homesickness and wanted to stay at Mesa Verde if he could not be transferred to an Oklahoma CCC camp. Finally, Taylor advised Mrs. Rice that her son's homesickness had been heightened by her claims that she missed him and her pleas that he seek a transfer to an Oklahoma camp. She should write cheerful letters, Taylor advised, adding that Lee's commanding officer praised him as a cooperative and willing worker.

sequences of misbehavior. They learned how to arrange their belongings, to make their beds, and to eat in the dining or mess hall. CCCers remember that they had initial adjustment problems as they established friendships or sometimes retreated into personal isolation.

Data from Company 1843 illustrates that in 1938, while some enrollees came from the same communities, others – notably from cities such as Denver, Pueblo, Corpus Christi and Ft. Worth – had few or no companions with the same place of origin. Thirty-five men (29 percent) were the only person from their hometown, and 56 percent of the communities represented in the camp had but a single enrollee.

Isolation in the camp was memorialized in a simple definition in the August 30 *Kiva Krier* which described a CCCer as "a guy what has a home but can't go there." Some enrollees, such as Arthur Wilson, nicknamed "Runt" by fellow CCCers, did live close enough to take weekend leave, and others would occasionally accompany them home. In mid-August of 1935 the "general assembly" of Camp 861 agreed to schedule the Saturday morning inspection at 6:30 a.m. to permit enrollees to leave after breakfast, but the policy necessitated that the boys rise by 5:30 on Saturdays to scrub the barracks.

Depending upon an enrollee's place of origin, the Mesa Verde altitude (nearly a mile above sea level) and extremes in temperature could create other adjustment problems. Park service temperature and precipitation records indicate that November through March generally were cold (the lowest temperatures were near single digits) and snowy (monthly snowfalls near 20 inches were common). Exposure to the elements at high altitude could also produce painful sunburn in summer as enrollees stripped off their shirts to work outside in the midday heat, and possible frostbite in winter if an enrollee misplaced his mittens.

Vermin, especially the famous Mesa Verde chipmunks, the notorious CCC bedbugs, and a plethora of cockroaches plagued men while they were in camp. While rodents undoubtedly caused problems by finding their way into the camp supplies, it was the seasonal attacks of bedbugs that provoked the most complaints. Less than a quarter of an inch in length, the blood-sucking insects did not spread disease, but their bites were very irritating, particularly in large numbers. CCC inspectors made formal visits in 1934, 1936, 1937, and 1941 to investigate complaints about the conditions in the Mesa Verde camps. Each visit resulted in a formal report prepared by the CCC external inspector and sent to the adjutant general in the War Department or to the director of the CCC.

In 1934, Captain Thomas F. Sheehan reported that both camps NP-5-C (Company 1843) and NP-6-C (Company 861) "were heavily infested with bedbugs and the kitchens are overrun with cockroaches." He reported that many enrollees complained about this situation. The bedbugs were a persistent problem that the authorities tried to combat by fumigating with cyanide gas (dropping cyanide capsules into cans filled with hydrochloric acid). In spite of the drastic treatment that forced the men to move outside or to share barracks for several days, the results were ineffective. Capt. Sheehan explained that various attempts to eliminate the bedbugs had failed because the bugs hibernated through the winters in the pinyon pines and cedar trees adjacent to the camp buildings. Certainly another source of re-infestation could be attributed to the arrival of new enrollees, who may have brought the bugs with them.

Three years later, J.C. Reddoch, special investigator, made a similar

COMMUNITIES OF ORIGIN
COMPANY 1843, CAMP NP-5-C MESA VERDE 1938

STATE OF ORIGIN	COMMUNITY	NUMBER OF ENROLLEES	STATE OF ORIGIN	COMMUNITY	NUMBER OF ENROLLEES
COLORADO			OKLAHOMA		
	Pueblo	1		Turley	1
	Mancos	4		Webber Falls	1
	Durango	2		Pittsburgh	2
	Lamar	1		Mounds	1
	Rocky Ford	1		Henryetta	6
	White Sulphur	1		Beggs	2
	Walsenburg	2		McAlester	7
	Denver	2		Adamson	3
	Lewis	1		Crowder	2
	Swink	3		Hartsthorne	7
	Antonito	5		Okmulgee	3
	Bayfield	1		Morris	4
	Fowler	1		Hoffman	1
	Dolores	1		Ti	1
	Pagosa Springs	2		Eufaula	2
	Cortez	2		Indianola	2
	La Junta	4		Haileyville	2
	Dove Creek	1		Kiowa	4
	Romeo	1		Beggs	2
	Dyke	1		Muldrow	1
	Alamosa	2		N. McAlester	2
	Jansen	1		Coalton	1
	San Luis	1		Lutie	1
	Arboles	1		Ateka	1
	Conejos	1		Caddo	1
	Yellow Jacket	2		Gans	1
TOTAL COLORADO		45		Vian	1
COLORADANS		37.5%		Wilburton	1
				Checotah	1
NEW MEXICO				Caney	1
	Lumberton	2		Blocker	1
	Taos	1	**TOTAL OKLAHOMA**		66
TOTAL NEW MEXICO		3	**OKLAHOMANS**		55.0%
NEW MEXICANS		2.5%			
			TEXAS		
				Jewett	1
				Corpus Christi	1
				Ft. Worth	1
			TOTAL TEXAS		3
			TEXANS		2.5%
			NO STATE LISTED		2.5%
			TOTAL COMPANY		120

report to J.J. McEntee, assistant director of the CCC. When he interviewed 40 enrollees in the Company 1843 recreation hall, he noted that all the men complained about the bedbugs.

> The bed-bug situation is terrible here. In the four barracks, I shook twenty-one cots and bed-bugs fell from twenty of them. Something should be done at once toward their extermination. Camps NP-5 and NP-6 are located very close together. Both camps are heavily infested with bed-bugs and it is my recommendation that the enrollees of one camp be quartered in the barracks of the other camp while the empty barracks are being fumigated.

He went on to note that the conditions were so bad that many men chose to sleep outside rather than stay in their vermin-infested cots. Enrollees remembered the periodic efforts at extermination, but the persistence of the complaints over time leaves little doubt that the CCC fought a losing battle against the insects in Mesa Verde.

External inspectors also provided useful detail about food served in the camps, reporting on menus during the week they were in the camps. From time to time the enrollees complained about the food, as evidenced by the humorous revision of a child's rhyme in the October 4, 1935, *Kiva Krier*.

> Enrollee Jack could eat no fats,
> His pal could eat no leans,
> Because they never had a chance,
> At anything but BEANS!

The enrollees, however, more often described their food supplies as plentiful and varied, but often not prepared well. A quick examination of the weekly menus documents a varied and generally balanced diet that included the basic food groups and almost certainly contained more plentiful portions and greater variety than enrollees experienced before joining the CCC. As a detailed menu in the appendix illustrates, the enrollees in the mid-1930s ate a plentiful supply of fresh fruits and vegetables (melons, grapefruit, oranges, berries, apples and fresh apple sauce, sweet and white potatoes, fresh corn, onions, radishes, peas, beans, cabbage, beets, spinach, carrots, cauliflower, tomatoes, cucumbers, and lettuce). According to the inspectors' reports, these supplies were bought on the open market, whereas meat, canned goods, and other dry staples came from the army quartermaster. With the hindsight of 50 years, enrollees reflecting upon their diet in the camps were more charitable in their recollections about the food and its preparation. They remembered it as plentiful, varied, and generally good.

Menus from 1936 and 1937 represent the mid-period in the CCC experience at Mesa Verde, and support the enrollees' comments regarding both the quantity and variety of food. In comparison to wartime army rations both earlier and later, these meals showed variety and careful attention to nutrition. If they are at all representative of what enrollees ate during their tenure in the Mesa Verde CCC camps, food was more plentiful, fresher, and more varied than the enrollees likely would have experienced before they accepted "relief work" with the CCC.

All meals were prepared under the auspices of the army. Breakfasts and suppers were served in camp mess halls, but army regulations for the camps presumably dictated that the men receive "hot dinners" convenient to their places of work. In an August 21, 1937, letter to James Reddoch, CCC special investigator, Park Superintendent Jesse L. Nusbaum complained that this practice was very inefficient and argued for a cold luncheon instead. He described luncheon procedures that prevailed from the first through the ninth enrollment period at Mesa Verde. If work groups were more than seven to eight miles from the camp headquarters, the army set up a central luncheon station, where a temporary building was erected, 12 picnic tables were assembled under protective canvas covers, and the meals were prepared on-site with the enrollees transported by pickup trucks to the midday mess site. The superintendent complained that this procedure was costly both in time lost and gasoline expended.

Nusbaum argued that the men preferred cold lunches, but the army resisted because meat and cheese sandwiches were more costly to prepare than the hot lunches. Furthermore, he claimed that hot lunches contributed to diminished work during the balance of each day. According to Nusbaum, only enrollees working in isolation – telephone operators and those doing pest control or seed collecting – received cold lunches.

In 1937 Inspector J.C. Reddoch also reported on other aspects of daily life in camp. Of the 139 men assigned to Company 1843, 21 (approximately 15 percent) were detailed to camp work, eight were sick or absent, and 110 (approximately 80 percent) were assigned to park work. The shoes for the men were "excellent," the mess hall, kitchen, officers' quarters, other buildings and camp area were "good," but the barracks were "poor."

As for camp sanitation, he noted that water was supplied by the deep well, which itself was a product of CCCers' work in the camp, and a major improvement for Mesa Verde National Park. Wastewater from the kitchen and bathing areas emptied into cesspools that were then drained through pipes into the canyon, about 300 feet from the camps. He described the latrines as "pit type," and indicated that the same design served the officers, the foremen, and the enrolled men. Garbage was hauled from the camps to the park's dumping ground daily. He also noted that the screen doors to the mess hall and the kitchen did not fit well, which permitted flies to enter the food preparation and service areas. The camp barbershop was not equipped with running water, and only neck shaves and haircuts were available for the enrollees.

According to a report of June 6, 1935, approximately a year after the first permanent camps were established at Mesa Verde, the amenities of camp NP-6-C included recreational equipment available for enrollees. Indoors, the men had a piano, a radio, ping-pong equipment, a woodcarving set, indoor balls, basketballs, checkerboards, a cribbage board, a chess set, domino sets, Monday Morning Coach (indoor football games), boxing gloves, a wrestling mat, basketball nets, and basketball suits and shoes. For outdoor use, there were football suits and shoes for 12, baseball suits and shoes for 15, volleyballs, volleyball nets, a football, baseball bats, and baseball gloves and equipment. Certainly within two years of the organization of the CCC, the permanent camps were obtaining recreation equipment so that the enrollees could continue to play the sports and games that they had known in their hometowns.

In 1936 Inspector Reddoch also queried the men about recreational opportunities outside the camp. He noted that the "Spanish" boys complained they were unwelcome in both Cortez and Mancos, which were the two most common destinations for trips away from the camps. These enrollees asked specifically for occasional trips to Durango, 65 miles away, which permitted them to interact socially with the local citizenry. The trips to town occurred every two to three weeks, which meant that the CCCers spent at least half of their time in camps on weekends in the mid-1930s. The reports about NP-5-C in both 1936 and 1937 detailed the recreational equipment available in the camp, including several additions: a pool table, cues and balls, writing desks, wood- and leather-working tools, card tables, army and navy songbooks, a soccer ball, softball supplies for an entire team, and horseshoes. Swimming trunks also were listed, although there was no place for CCCers to swim in the park. The camps offered a wide range of recreational outlets for the enrollees, a result of efforts to improve both the camp facilities and recreational opportunities.

By October 23, 1941, Earnest Dugas made the last recorded inspection trip to the Mesa Verde CCC campsite, four years after Company 1843 had been consolidated with Company 861, leaving only one CCC camp at Mesa Verde. The economic recovery that followed the beginning of World War II in September 1939 had made the CCC a less attractive alternative for young men seeking work; hence company strength had fallen to 110. Meanwhile there had been dramatic improvements in the camp services. Dugas described the buildings as properly maintained, and reported that the camp water supply from the National Park Service was tested monthly by Fitzsimons General Hospital, a military hospital in Denver. The pit latrines had been replaced by a flush system with sewer lines that was used by both enrollees and officers. The camp buildings were heated by coal and the buildings were "properly maintained." Dugas reported that the camp itself was in good order.

Originally, each Mesa Verde CCC camp had its own medical officer, but by 1941 the declining CCC enrollment, improved transportation, Congressional budget cuts, and the demands of pre-war preparedness prompted cutbacks in medical services. The remaining camp was one of four served by a doctor. Men continued to be tested for venereal diseases monthly and now food handlers were tested every other week for cleanliness and infectious diseases. Meat supplies were inspected by a veterinarian, and all perishable foods were refrigerated. Dugas reported that company morale was excellent, as were enrollees' shoes, clothes, canteen, barracks, kitchen, mess hall, officers' quarters, technical staff quarters, the infirmary, the supply room, the garages, the oil house, the education building, the bath house, the latrine, the camp area, the laundry and the records and activity center. Food supplies, the mess and the recreation hall were all rated "superior."

In addition to the recreation supplies and opportunities mentioned in the 1937 report, men now had picture shows, wrestling and boxing matches, and weekly trips to town. There was also more attention paid to religious instruction, which was now available weekly with the chaplain visiting the camp twice per month. Dugas had a few important recommendations, but they paled in comparison with the bedbug and cockroach concerns voiced by his predecessors. He suggested that beds be made up fresh daily, that expenses for laundry were too great, that the new green uniforms be pressed, that dishes not be dried with towels, but rather allowed to drain from the sterilizer, and that dish pans rather than pitchers be used for cleaning the tables.

When the legislation of 1937 officially re-named the ECW the Civilian Conservation Corps, it gave new impetus to the educational mission of the CCC. The focus was clearly reflected in the questions inspector Dugas addressed in his report, noting for the first time what subjects were offered in classes at Mesa Verde. Enrollees could take high school coursework in arithmetic, reading, English, geography, history, civics, psychology, hygiene, woodworking, American government, leatherwork, cooking and baking, typing, and auto mechanics. The camp leaders also offered vocational instruction in career education, first aid, safety education, road construction, leadership, conservation, carpentry, PBX switchboard operation, truck driving, blacksmithing, tractor operation, and surveying.

The success of the educational work was captured in a typical CCC summary of accomplishments. During the preceding year the camps in the park and in Mancos had issued 38 eighth-grade diplomas and 75 first aid certificates; and enrollees had received 80 proficiency certificates, 78 unit certificates, two college scholarships, and 12 job placements.

The camp chaplains served a similar role in providing the enrollees with moral and ethical guidance to help them form the habits that would later guide their lives. The August 23, 1935, *Kiva Krier* reported on two recent visits by the chaplains. The first, Chaplain McCaddon, stressed the importance of self-respect and appropriate temperance in talk and drink. Swearing and drinking were not the marks of a morally responsible man, he counseled. The second, Chaplain Leach, stressed the importance of establishing good habits which in turn shaped one's character, guided one's career and ultimately defined one's destiny. Chaplain Leach advised the men to reject the bad acts that often appealed to them. By choosing good behavior daily the men adopted good habits of thought and action, and so laid the foundation for a successful life, he said.

Enrollees in the Mesa Verde CCC camps had daily leisure time once they completed their workday and ate their supper. Normally this was several hours each night. In the summer the men walked around in the evenings or took walks to the ruins. They could always go to the recreation hall, usually "rec hall" for short, where they could purchase toiletries, cigarettes, and candy at the camp canteen. They could also play various games: pool, indoor football, checkers, dominoes, poker, and such.

One enrollee remembered that he spent most of his spare time playing matchstick poker. Because gambling was banned, the men used matchsticks instead of money, but in reality they kept track of their losses. This enrollee remembered sadly that as a youth in Cheyenne, Wyoming, he had learned how to deal from the bottom of the deck, and so was able to add to his monthly wage of $5 by cheating in poker. "It was easy," he remarked, wistfully condemning himself for cheating his poor rural companions out of their monthly allotments.

In the first half of the 20th century, young men found boxing a popular means of demonstrating their physical prowess. In the Southwest Region, with several major CCC camps, boxing became a way to pit camps against one another. In the November 1935 Company 1843 newsletter the *Mesa Verdian* touted the impending boxing match at the Gem Theater where Joe Stepan, Joe Roybal, and One-Round Guthrie from Mesa Verde Company 1843 would compete against teams of 10 to 12 fighters from Durango and Redmesa. Though the outcome of the boxing matches on Friday, November 8, 1935, are not recorded in the scattered surviving issues of the *Mesa Verdian* the spirit of those long lost conflicts reminds us of a time when young men's physical prowess defined their masculinity.

While boxing was an individual sport emphasizing strength, football, baseball, and basketball were team sports that occasioned competition between the enrollees of Companies 1843 and 861, as well as with neighboring camps in southwestern Colorado. The October 11, 1935, *Kiva Krier* reported the results of the football game between Company 861 and Durango's CCC camp. The Mesa Verde boys lost 32 to 0. Two enrollees suffered injuries: Percy Pino, associate editor of the *Kiva Krier,* suffered twisted ligaments in his arm and a CCCer named Evans broke several bones in his hand. Lt. Thomas, the Company 861 commander, commended his team for their spirit of fair play and good sportsmanship. He said the 861 team lost not because of lack of effort, but because the Durango team "showed more training." He concluded: "Winning isn't the only thing that counts; it's the attitude that you show, and what you put in that matters." Though Thomas affirmed sportsmanship as the great accomplishment of the game, two weeks later the *Kiva Krier* reported that in their meeting at Mesa Verde, the camp commanders decided to outlaw football in the CCC camps in the southwestern Colorado area. Perhaps the fate of Pino and Evans contributed to this decision.

Though now remembered as one of the New Deal's remarkable accomplishments, in its own time the CCC and its enrollees often had "the reputation of being ruffians, nere-do-wells, etc.," to use the description of CCC boys presented by the editor of Company 861's *Kiva Krier* (October 25, 1935). Editor Platt Cline disputed the assumptions of the CCC's critics and even some of the CCCers, maintaining that the CCC enrollees had distinguished themselves as men willing to work rather than "living off someone else." The enrollees, he argued, had contributed to society by making a living and helping to employ others. They were men between the ages of 18 and 25 when they enrolled, men who worked hard and made a living, while helping their families. Was it a disgrace to earn a living? According to Cline it certainly was not; those who had enrolled in the CCC had become productive citizens. He concluded that those who prided themselves upon being roughnecks would certainly have earned that reputation whether they were in the CCC or not.

Throughout the summer and fall of 1935 the *Kiva Krier* reported weekly on the recreational opportunities in nearby Mancos. Mr. Gollogher operated the Mancos Theatre, which served as both movie theater and occasional dance hall. On August 2, the *Kiva Krier* listed the films that would be shown in Mancos – Will Rogers in *The County Chairman*, Donald Woods and Margaret Lindsay in *The Florentine Dagger*, and Jeanette MacDonald and Nelson Eddy in *Naughty Marietta*. The article on the movies also noted that there was a regular discount for enrollees at the theater.

There was also a dance on the evening of August 2 that featured Ernie Anderson's Band, which the *Kiva Krier* reported was a favorite among the CCCers in the Mesa Verde area. The following week Company 861's officers and their wives chaperoned a dance in the mess hall at the camp, which cost the enrollees 50 cents, the standard charge in the fall of 1935, but advertised ladies were free! It didn't specify where the "ladies" would come from, but presumably they were from Mancos or Cortez. One feature of the evening event was the performance of the picturesque and popular tango by Señorita Primorosa Bailadora and Señor Benito de Herrera, who danced to the music of Señor Enrique Ybarra. One week after the dance, the August 16 *Kiva Krier* reported that it had been "quite a doings." The organizers had a cash balance after all expenses had been paid, and the editor wondered, "Why not have a dance here at least once or twice a month?"

"Observer's" View

Non-CCC visitors to the park occasionally commented on their impressions of both the park and the work of the enrollees. The August 2, 1935, edition of the *Kiva Krier* published an account of one Rock Springs visitor who signed himself "an observer" and accompanied the CCC forestry foreman and his reconstruction crew to the area on Wetherill Mesa which had been the scene of the Great Mesa Verde fire of 1934. The observer, likely a community leader or official, described the scene.

> Devastation!!! Devastation vast, utter and complete! To our right, to our left, and before us, mile after mile of blackened stumps, ghost-like remains of what had once been beautiful rolling verdure-covered mesa land! Now without a vestige of living green upon its face!

He reported that the park service had begun three major restoration projects: reseeding, reforestation, and erosion control. When he visited the park, the enrollees were engaged in the final part of the project, the erosion control. Though he explained that he had often heard complaints about the CCC laced with terms such as "chiseling, suction and gold-bricking," he was pleased to report that he had seen none on his day at the fire scene.

> No "Gold-bricking" here. Sand and dust, hot winds and hotter sun, wearing work with axe and cross-cut saw; but throughout the day, never a sign of a gold-bricker, a panty-waist, a chocolate covered creampuff ... A temper-testing task in the sizzling heat of summer, this falling and trimming of charred, tough stumps and trees, to prevent the thin dry soil being blown across the hills into the San Juan River!

Nearly all enrollees took occasional tours of the ruins in the national park. On Sunday, August 18, 1935, Paul Franke, the park naturalist, led a group of 19 enrollees from Company 861 into Fewkes Canyon near the Sun Temple. Though the boys enjoyed the chance to tour some of the less often visited ruins, *Kiva Krier* Editor Platt Cline reported that Franke encouraged them to arrange their tours for Saturdays in the future, because Sundays were the days in which the park had its most visitors. Sundays were also occasions for visits by enrollees from other camps. On Sunday, August 18, 1935, 70 men came to Mesa Verde from the Redmesa camp and on Sunday, October 13, 1935, 16 enrollees from the Norwood camp came to Mesa Verde.

Holidays undoubtedly posed special challenges for the enrollees at Mesa Verde, because these were times when their minds turned naturally to childhood and hometown experiences. During the 1930s the United States citizens in the West and Southwest celebrated a select group of secular and religious holidays – the New Year, Valentine's Day, Independence Day, Labor Day, Halloween, Armistice Day, Thanksgiving, and Christmas.

The August 30, 1935, *Kiva Krier* described the Labor Day celebration planned by the Mancos American Legion. Enrollees received time off for this holiday, and all were invited to Mancos to join in the festivities. Activities began at 9 a.m. with a parade that offered prizes for various categories of entrants. It was followed by a band concert, and then a baseball game in Boyle Park. Another concert followed the baseball game, and then there was a rodeo at the fairgrounds. As with the parade, there were $100 prizes for the best performances in the steer- and calf-roping contests. After the rodeo two airplane pilots would demonstrate airplane stunts and fancy flying. The pilots also promised to take passengers for rides after the exhibition of flying skills. In the early evening the American Legion planned a 7:30 p.m. boxing program that featured Abe Chavez of Towaoc against Kayo Short from Brownwood, Texas. The preliminary program included CCC fights pitting Joe Rovil of Company 1843 against Frenchy Ancil of Company 898 from Beaver (near Dolores), Link Austin against Slugging Kid, and Charlie Murray against Battler Roack of Beaver. Predictably, the day's entertainment concluded with dances at both the Mancos Theatre and the I.O.O.F. Hall.

Though Halloween had religious roots, it had become a thoroughly secular holiday in the first half of the 20th century. The November 6, 1935, edition of the *Mesa Verdian* reported on the "second Halloween blowout" for Company 1843. The officers and men joined together in the frivolity as Lt. M.K. Ledbetter and the other leaders Lt. J.C. Creel, Lt. Col. E.G. Condit (physician) and *Mesa Verdian* editors C.W. Phillips and Sammy Johnson coordinated the festivities. Like most Halloween parties, this one combined seasonal food with a challenging variation on the traditional apple-bobbing contests. The coordinators suspended an apple on a string from the rafters into a G.I. boiler filled with salty water. Successful contestants were awarded a pack of cigarettes from the four cartons used as prizes for the event. Overall the enrollees consumed "fifty-five gallons of cider, three bushels of apples, boilers of doughnuts, and three bushels of popcorn." One can only wonder if the popcorn was popped or seeds! Enrollee and *Mesa Verdian* cartoonist Pete Martinez memorialized the evening in a November 6, 1935, cartoon entitled "Our Halloween Party Featuring Lts. Ledbetter, Creel, and the Colonel." The three officers are depicted dancing on stage while an enrollee with a cup in his hand slumps on the apple- and doughnut-littered floor beside a barrel labeled "cider" and a smaller box labeled "more cider."

Thanksgiving was another important holiday in the camps. In keeping with the tradition established by Abraham Lincoln during the Civil War, the men in Companies 1843 and 861 held festive dinners on Thanksgiving. Enrollee George Stithen of Company 1843 remembered Thanksgiving as the one time each year when food was served family style. The meal was a Thanksgiving feast with turkey and all of the trimmings. Though he remembered the camp food as being consistently plentiful, tasty and nutritious, the Thanksgiving dinner was a memorable event for young enrollees. The lavish spread contrasted sharply with what many of the CCC boys had experienced on the Thanksgiving preceding their enrollment. The combination of the good food, coupled with the knowledge that their monthly stipend provided $25 for their families, seemed the basis for real thanks in an era of privation and uncertainty.

Christmas and New Year's, too, were occasions for celebration and good food. The December 1935 *Cliff Dweller*, the newly created joint newspaper for both camps, reported the respective Christmas menus for companies 1843 and 861. Both mess halls served "roast young turkey," fruit salad, bread and butter, nuts, and milk and coffee, but there the similarity stopped. Company 1843 received apple dressing, candied sweet potatoes, baked corn, cranberry sauce, buttered peas, mashed potatoes, combination salad, pie a la mode, cocoa and candy. Their counterparts in 861 enjoyed chicken soup, giblet gravy, pickles, potato rosetta, oyster dressing, celery, tomatoes, string beans, onions, pickled beets, pumpkin pie, and mince pie, topped off with cigars and cigarettes.

In 1936 there were more food items in common as both companies enjoyed turkey, oyster dressing, hot rolls and butter, cranberry sauce, candied yams, mince and pumpkin pies, plum pudding, French drip coffee, and fruits, nuts, and candies of the season. Company 861 had mashed potatoes, fruit salad, baked corn, fruitcake and chocolate cake, whereas Company 1843 enjoyed cream pea soup, giblet gravy, cheese mound potatoes, buttered peas, assorted pickles, celery hearts, chow chow, and nut loaf cake. Not all of the enrollees were present for the Christmas spread or the New Year meal because half the men received five-day furloughs that began on December 21 and ended December 26, whereas the others began their furloughs on December 28 and returned on January 2. The *Cliff Dweller* in 1935 noted that the furloughs allowed the men to drop their picks and shovels and go home to report on the accomplishments of the two camps at Mesa Verde. Project Superintendent J.J. Drennan of Company 1843 reported that most of the men in camp "availed themselves of the opportunity to spend their Christmas holidays at home."

In coordinating the daily life in the CCC camps, the officers and CCCers themselves attempted to create a lifestyle that was similar to that lived before men came to the CCC. If there was adequate food, shelter, a sanitary environment, and typical leisure-time activities, company morale was better and the isolation of Mesa Verde less distressing to the young men who were often far from home and friends. By contrast, when bedbugs, poor or inadequate food, and separation or discrimination were common, the CCCers individually or collectively were more dissatisfied with their lives. While park and camp officials could affect the life in camp, the CCCers were expected to provide a day's work for a day's pay, and their tasks were usually labor-intensive and characteristically unglamorous.

6

"The New Spirit of the American Future"

An overview of the 1933 Civilian Conservation Corps camp that was located in Prater Canyon.

T hey were called the "Tree Army," the young men of the Civilian Conservation Corps. Between 18 and 25 years of age at the time of enrollment, unemployed and unmarried, they enlisted for six months at $30 per month. Especially in the early years, many renewed their enrollment beyond the first six months.

Mesa Verde's camps were in the eighth district and among nearly 50 located in national parks, including Rocky Mountain National Park in Colorado. President Franklin Roosevelt held high hopes for what the CCC would accomplish for these fellows. In a radio speech on July 17, 1933, he told them.

> Men of the Civilian Conservation Corps, I think of you as a visible token of encouragement to the whole country.
>
> It is time for each and every one of us to cast away self-destroying, nation-destroying efforts to get something for nothing, and to appreciate that satisfying rewards come only through honest work.
>
> That must be the new spirit of the American future. You are the vanguard of that new spirit.

Mesa Verde National Park

Tents and jerry-built buildings were home for the CCCers at the first campsite.

July 1933 enrollees pose for their group photo.

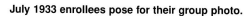

Mesa Verde National Park

The "bug crew" stops for a moment before venturing out to curb
beetle and tent caterpillar infestations.

The boys starting off at 7:45 a.m. for a day's work in the park.

Part of the crew that fought the Wild Horse Mesa and Wickiup fires in July 1934.

CCC barracks were ready for inspection; after all, the military ran the camps.

Boys getting cleaned up. Soon after this photo was taken, the camp wash house was completed.

Physical fitness and recreation were an important aspect of the CCC.

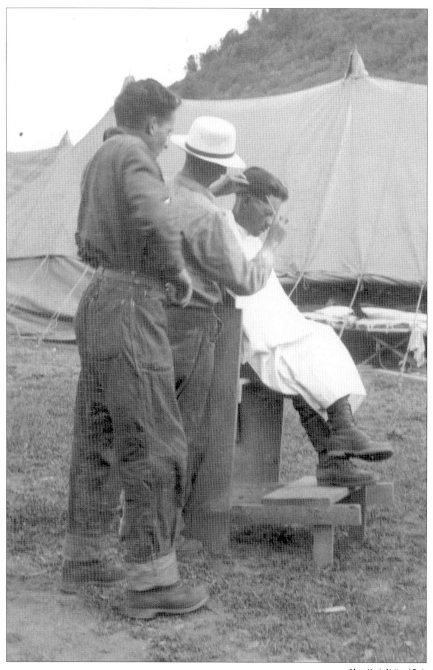

**Not quite the barbershop in their old hometown,
but just as effective.**

Mesa Verde National Park

**Perhaps nothing was more eagerly anticipated than meals, after which
the plates had to be cleaned.**

7

The CCC Legacy –
Three-Quarters of a Century Later

W ithin a year of the arrival of permanent companies 861 and 1843 in 1934, Park Superintendent Ernest P. Leavitt asked the director of the National Park Service for approval to continue winter work at the two Mesa Verde CCC camps. He explained that the Public Works projects initiated in 1933-34 were the initial justification for a year-round construction program in the park. Though the winter of 1934-35 had been severe, the supervisory personnel had operated the camps all winter thanks to several make-up work sessions. By early August 1935, Leavitt reported that the presence of both the Public Works projects and the CCC camps in the park, had, in two years, advanced the Mesa Verde master plan more than he could have anticipated in a decade. Under normal conditions park projects were approved in the amount of a few thousand dollars per year. But with year-round work crews and a dramatically increased project budget, Leavitt asked for permission to add projects to the master plan. In the brief span of two years Mesa Verde had changed from a small seasonal park to "a full fledged all around construction park." As Leavitt understood, the CCC had already transformed his park.

Seven months later returning Park Superintendent Jesse L. Nusbaum told J.C. Roak, ECW representative of the Eighth Corps Area at Fort Sam Houston, Texas, that there were sufficient incomplete projects and newly proposed ones to keep two camps busy in Mesa Verde.

In 1938 Associate Director of the National Park Service A.E. Demaray asked the park superintendents to comment upon the CCC work. Nusbaum responded March 9, explaining the CCC's extraordinary accomplishments in Mesa Verde National Park, which he described as one of the "older national parks." He labeled Mesa Verde "world famous," and stressed the important changes that had come to the park since the establishment of two CCC camps in the summer of 1934. He credited the CCC with helping bring about those changes by adding to visitors' comfort and enhancing their enjoyment of the park. He singled out as notable the campground improvements which prompted a four-fold increase in campground visitors (20 to 80) and a three-fold increase in the number of visitors who could attend the evening campfire presentations (80 to 250). He commended also an improved aesthetic appearance of the park and the accommodations that it provided both its resident and seasonal employees. Furthermore CCC enrollees had participated broadly in the park activities, serving as assistants in the offices, museum, and public contact points in the park. The work of the CCC at Mesa Verde constituted a lasting contribution to the park and a monument to the Civilian Conservation Corps, he concluded.

The program had proven to be an economic windfall for the national park, since CCC manpower and funds supplemented park funds, expanding the potential for improvements. Nusbaum enthusiastically asserted that if it were continued for an additional decade, Mesa Verde National Park would continue the remarkable physical improvement it had experienced in the preceding four years. To prove his point, he offered a long list of projects that could be initiated in a decade:

- checking station at the park entrance
- construction of comfort stations throughout the park
- creation of a larger picnic area and campground
- creation of fire lookouts
- enlargement of the campfire circle
- improvement of the communication system
- installation of underground electrical connections
- addition of guardrails and curbing in the headquarters area
- construction of new foot trails
- completion of firetruck trails
- repair and alterations of park housing
- improvement of the Prater Canyon maintenance camp
- minor road work
- development of water supplies in Navajo, White, and Waters canyons
- expansion of the water storage reservoir
- replacement of frame buildings with masonry ones
- erection of a permanent pump house
- construction of stock buildings for the pack and saddle operator
- additional road sloping and obliteration of abandoned or temporary roads

Nusbaum's enthusiasm was understandable: The CCC could continue to be very good for the park, for years to come.

Leavitt's and Nusbaum's conclusions demonstrated that the CCC immediately changed Mesa Verde and the public's perception of the park and its facilities. But Nusbaum's dream of continued help was not to be. With the war looming, the program dwindled to only 76 enrollees at the end of February 1942, the last month for which a formal report from Superintendent Townsend survives. When the last men left in 1942, their camps became ghost communities. Having lost his labor force, Nusbaum attempted to at least retain control of CCC equipment for the park. The CCC supplies had significantly augmented the park's resources, but he lost this battle, too. By fall 1942 the War Department was gradually securing all the mechanical equipment except for light tools, specialized devices, and useless vehicles. The War Department requisitioned even such items as a loose-leaf binder, two pen sets and eight pair of pliers. None of the supplies was seen as more important to a rubber-starved army than the 184 CCC tires held by Mesa Verde. One need only remember that the national gasoline rationing during World War II was less important for gasoline saved than the scarce rubber tires which it preserved.

Only obsolete, useless or worn-out implements such as axes, block and tackle, surveyor's compasses, picks, rakes, scythes, shovels, and such stayed in the park. The War Department even considered dismantling the barracks for salvage parts as the country became fully mobilized for World War II. In most camps the records were discarded or shipped off to the War Department and then to the National Archives. Because its missions were anthropological and historical, Mesa Verde's superintendents preserved its CCC resources, but as camp buildings deteriorated and its remaining vehicles were abandoned, the CCC slipped from public memory both in the park and in the nation.

The CCC legacy was ignored during the war years. Afterward the nation entered a new era of prosperity and international commitment, paying little heed to the CCC legacy for almost 20 years. The ideology of the early Cold War era emphasized individualism and capitalism, while minimizing the social cooperation that caused President Roosevelt to create agencies such as the CCC. Interest in the New Deal and its agencies reemerged in the late 1950s and, especially in the 1960s as Democratic Presidents Kennedy and Johnson reexamined the accomplishments of the New Deal. President Johnson, who had been a youthful New Dealer and National Youth Administration official in Texas, looked back to the inspiration of the New Deal when he launched his "War on Poverty." One of the direct consequences was his creation of the Job Corps, which promised to teach job skills to urban, poor, at-risk youth while relocating them to special camps that were remote from the environment of poverty.

...THE CCC BROUGHT DECADES OF PROGRESS TO THE NATIONAL PARKS IN A MERE NINE YEARS.

In the 1930s, CCC critics complained about enrollees' work ethic, honesty, and personal morality. By contrast, men who had served in the camps remembered their companions as basically hard-working ("few gold brickers" was their refrain), conscientious, well-intentioned, and grateful. Contemporary commentators praised the CCC's conservation work which ameliorated the consequences of the drought of the 1950s, when the tree breaks and water retention initiatives reduced the damage that had accompanied the drought of the 1930s. At the same time, park visitors marveled over the various improvements that the corps had made. As Leavitt and Nusbaum acknowledged early on, the CCC brought decades of progress to the national parks in a mere nine years.

Comparing both the earlier and later government funding commitments to the parks illustrates clearly the importance of the CCC contributions of both money and manpower for buildings, infrastructure, roads, forest management, and visitor conveniences. From the 1980s onward Mesa Verde recognized the CCC contributions and encouraged former CCCers to return to the site of their youthful work. Mesa Verde Superintendent Robert Heyder promoted the annual "old timers" picnics and encouraged all who had worked in the park to return each fall. He placed advertisements in area newspapers and organized a CCC reunion in the park. Simultaneously, CCCers themselves became interested in their common heritage and organized national and regional associations of former enrollees, who visited the locations that shaped their young lives.

In interviews with local residents who spent time in the CCC on Mesa Verde, it became clear that few ever used the skills they learned "on the job" at Mesa Verde. One enrollee pointed with pride to a bricked flower bed and claimed it was his first and only masonry work done in the ensuing half century. Another remembered that he began cutting hair in the rec hall to earn a little money and turned this into his vocation. A third credited the CCC with introducing him to the National Park Service, where he worked after the war until his retirement. This was consistent with the original intent of the Emergency Conservation Work Act, but it didn't fulfill the expectations of some CCC supporters. They wanted men to learn job skills they could use after leaving the CCC. Although they may not have learned trades while in the CCC, most men said they did learn discipline and the importance of hard work in the camps. Others believe the pre-war military training component taught them military discipline, which led to early promotions in the wartime army. Almost all CCCers credited their CCC experience with giving them hope when their situations seemed desperate. One enrollee explained it succinctly, saying that but for the CCC, he would have been in a penitentiary.

8

A Walking Tour of CCC Sites

By Don Ross

T oday's visitors to Mesa Verde National Park unknowingly see many of the results from nine years of Civilian Conservation Corps projects in the park. While projects were undertaken throughout the park, it is the results of their efforts in the headquarters area that are most visible. Since this is the primary area that most park visitors spend time in and around, let's focus on the historic "center" of Mesa Verde National Park.

In actuality, almost everywhere we walk, park, view or spend time while in the museum/administration area, we can see and even touch some of the CCC boys' accomplishments. So let's take a little walk around this historic area and discover some of the CCC legacy.

Of all the extensive work performed in the museum area some would say the most important project was the museum building itself. Without a doubt, the single most noticed (and noteworthy) project built by CCC workers is the set of fabulous dioramas depicting the activities of Ancestral Puebloans of the Mesa Verde area.

Since the dioramas and their development are more than adequately covered in another section of this volume, let us be content to acknowledge and admire them and move on to other features of the museum which were built or improved during the CCC era.

A few steps past the diorama hallway are the museum auditorium, offices, and an extensive basement containing more offices and storage facilities for both NPS and Mesa Verde Museum Association staff. This area is the "nerve center" and home-away-from-home for the interpretation rangers and staff, as well as the bookstore folks. This area along with the exhibit rooms, lobby, and open courtyard in the center are all parts of a major expansion of the original museum building, a planned NPS project that was completed in 1936. Almost all the excavation, construction, masonry work and finishing details were performed by CCC boys under CCC supervision along with National Park Service advisers.

Venturing back outside, let's look around at more facilities and amenities built or improved by CCC fellows.

First, look closely at the road area. Notice the expertly cut and placed stone curbing all along the drive. Next we'll walk over to the small parking lot directly across from the museum. This was one of many important, needed park improvements done during the first year of CCC work projects. Notice the stonework of the curbs and the island in the center, particularly the three-foot stone wall that encircles almost the whole parking area. All of the very finely cut pieces of sandstone which we see here and all around the headquarters area were produced from a quarry in the park developed by CCC crews. During the nine years (1933-1942) of CCC activities, tons of rock were mined, cut into needed sizes, and hauled to various areas in the park.

Now, let's walk a little farther to the west and see a place few visitors are even aware of. A few yards west of the main park road, situated at the edge of Spruce Canyon is the Chapin Mesa Amphitheatre. This beautiful facility was another much needed improvement during the park's "growing years." Mesa Verde was the first national park to provide a campfire program for visitors, today a longtime tradition of the NPS. By the 1930s a larger and better place than the old fire circle with benches near the museum was required to provide this important component of the park's educational activities. This amphitheater is another striking example of the benefits of the ECW program at Mesa Verde. A natural bowl in the landscape was transformed into the fantastic spot we admire today. From the late 1930s through the 1960s the amphitheater was alive with activities. Ranger-naturalist campfire talks and traditional Navajo dances performed by park Navajo workers were outstanding highlights of activities that took place here. Unfortunately, this wonderful facility is not utilized presently, except for special occasions. Over the years, numerous weddings of park personnel and other local folks have occurred at this beautiful location.

MOST OF THE TRAILS, WALKWAYS, AND ROADS, AS WELL AS LANDSCAPING OF THE WHOLE HEADQUARTERS AREA, WERE ... ACCOMPLISHED BY THE CAPABLE, STRONG YOUNG MEN OF THE CCC.

As we wander back toward the museum and parking area, we can see and appreciate more of the CCC legacy. Most of the trails, walkways, and roads, as well as landscaping of the whole headquarters area – including the transplanting of native trees, shrubs, plants and grasses – were all part of the park's program of improvements accomplished by the capable, strong young men of the CCC.

Other locations near "park central" (museum/headquarters loop) built by CCCers, or improved during the heyday of the ECW/CCC program include: the peaceful picnic area (originally the park campground), five stone hogans constructed for Navajo park employees and their families, 19 housekeeping cabins for seasonal and permanent park staff, and many, many other more subtle works.

Another important CCC project that can be seen by park visitors today, but beyond the scope of this walking tour, is the fire lookout tower located at the highest place in the park – Park Point. At an altitude of 8,572 feet, Park Point provides a 360-degree view for over a hundred miles of the Four Corners area. Park staff, as well as CCC workers had utilized the location to watch for "smokes" or any signs of willdfire for some time; however, a permanent up-to-date facility was needed. A designated CCC project then began and the lookout tower still in use today was constructed during one season.

Park visitors with an interest in the CCC legacy at Mesa Verde should plan a short visit to Park Point, 10 miles north of the museum area. Traveling back toward Morefield campground, a marked turnout leads a short distance to the Park Point parking area. From the parking lot, a short walk up the marked path brings visitors to the fire lookout tower and one of the most impressive panoramic views anywhere in the Four Corners region.

As Ricardo Torres-Reyes wrote in his *Mesa Verde National Park, an Administrative History, 1906-1970,* the impact of New Deal programs on the park was profound and far-reaching.

> It is almost impossible to single out one park activity that was not affected by the help of Public Works, Emergency Construction and Emergency Construction Work money. Work of lasting and permanent character, amounting to thousands of dollars in value and work that otherwise would have probably remained undone for many years for want of appropriations was completed in the park. The CCC was everywhere: road building, landscaping, furniture making, restoration of vegetation, pest control, development of camp sites, construction of buildings, electrical work; assisting as guides, store clerks, office clerks, mechanics, fire lookouts, fire fighters, museum work, ranger assistants, pump operators – all and a lot more jobs performed by enrollees in the CCC – young men learning trades as they performed their work.

As appreciative lovers of this unique, fabulous national park of the "Green Table," we should be eternally grateful for the legacy of "Roosevelt's Tree Army" – the young men of the Civilian Conservation Corps.

(*Don Ross is the son of Kenneth Ross, who worked for the CCC in Mesa Verde as an LEM on such diverse projects as construction of the museum dioramas and publication of the camp newspapers. He went on to work as a seasonal ranger in the park and was the park naturalist during World War II. Don also was a park ranger for 12 years and developed an extensive research file and illustrated presentation on the CCC in Mesa Verde.*)

9

ARCHITECTURE, DESIGN AND CONSTRUCTION
OF CCC CAMPS AT MESA VERDE

BY SUSANA M. JONES

T he architecture and layout of the Civilian Conservation Corps (CCC) camps at Mesa Verde is representative of the utilitarian and military style of design and construction of the United States War Department during the early years of the CCC. The camps were constructed and operated under the direction of the United States Army in typical military manner.

The first CCC camps in Colorado were organized and built in a haphazard fashion due to lack of time, wet spring conditions, and lack of prior experience in organization and construction of such camps. As the program became better organized, so did the camps. Staff for the camps was hired immediately after the CCC was formed in April 1933 and troops for Mesa Verde's first camp, NP-2, began arriving the following month. In the beginning, the Colorado District Army Commander allowed the staff officer at each Colorado camp to decide how to best construct an adequate camp in the shortest amount of time, while staying within the allotted budget for labor and materials. As a result of the wet spring weather, good building materials were difficult to obtain.

Contrary to federal directives, the first camp at Mesa Verde was built by the CCC enrollees. Federal procedures stated that, "Enrollees of the Civilian Conservation Corps will not be used in the construction of buildings of a permanent or semi-permanent nature except temporarily in an emergency which does not permit obtaining other labor." It was a necessary constraint, because local communities benefited from the demand for labor and materials needed to construct the CCC camps. Using local labor, tradesmen, and materials was important for good public relations, and would help ensure the acceptance of CCC camps by the people in nearby communities.

Since the staff officer at each camp was allowed to decide how to construct the camps in the beginning of the CCC era, none of the initial Colorado camps resembled one another. By September 1933, when the army had become better organized in CCC camp design and construction, the captain of the 2nd Engineers at Fort Logan, Colorado, began assigning army officers from the base to be responsible for construction at each camp, assisted by a civilian construction superintendent.

After the first enrollment, things were no longer as rushed or disorganized, and Colorado camps were then constructed using civilian tradesmen and laborers. Even though the CCC crews did not do any construction work on the Mesa Verde camps after the first one was erected in spring 1933, they did do ground- and road-clearing in preparation for the construction of permanent camps.

DESIGN AND LAYOUT

Camp layout and building design were based on War Department guidelines. Mesa Verde's first Civilian Conservation Corps camp – NP-2 in Prater Canyon – initially was erected as a temporary camp, using military tents that housed offices, kitchen, mess hall and barracks. While most of the men at NP-2 were quartered in tents, there were also two small barracks. Temporary camps were established for a period not to exceed 18 months, but not all temporary camps were military tent camps. The early tent camps were intended to be replaced by wooden structures that could be easily dismantled and re-erected. However, NP-2 was abandoned in the summer of 1934 after an extremely harsh winter.

CCC tent camps were typically built to be used until wood buildings could be assembled, but were sometimes used as permanent shelters where the weather was conducive to year-round tent living. Camps were designed to accommodate from 25 to 200 men. Prater NP-2 was intended to become a "rigid" camp until it was determined the canyon was too wet to be suitable. It was not a surprise to the Mesa Verde chief ranger, who had warned the army that Prater Canyon was too damp and disagreeable for a camp.

Since the Prater Canyon location was not well suited to a year-round camp, NP-2 was supplanted by NP-5 and NP-6 when they were established in 1934 on Chapin Mesa. The location of the two permanent camps was only one-half mile north of the Mesa Verde park headquarters. Some of the material from the abandoned NP-2 camp was used by the army for sheeting at the new camps. Usable material not needed for the new camps was turned over to the National Park Service to be salvaged for use on NPS property.

In the fall of 1937, as enrollment dropped, NP-6 merged into the NP-5 location and it would be the one remaining camp at Mesa Verde. Before the merger of the camps, Park Superintendent Jesse Nusbaum recommended that NP-5 was a better location than NP-6 for the combined camp. Nusbaum's reasoning was that the recreation hall was nicer, the camp was closer to the recreation area, snow removal was easier, and the water supply was furnished from a nearby 85,000-gallon reservoir, next to the deep water well. Combining the two camps included a plan to partially dismantle some of the NP-6 buildings and use the material to build an education center for the combined camps. The buildings that were chosen to remain or be moved to NP-5 were refurbished before the men moved in; cost for the rehabilitation of NP-5 was approximately $1,500.

In April of 1938 the unused buildings and equipment from the consolidation of the camps were turned over to the park by the army:

1 Headquarters Building	160' x 20'
1 Mess Hall and Kitchen	176' x 20'
1 Recreation Hall	96' x 20'
5 Barracks	112' x 20'
1 Bath House	62' x 20'

Plus doors, windows, heaters, plumbing fixtures, light fixtures, and fire equipment

The park did not have a use for all the buildings and later returned three of the barracks and the headquarters building to the army. Although the CCC crews were not allowed to construct the camps, the CCC men spent 657 days tearing down and stacking lumber from the old NP-6 buildings.

The layout for NP-5 was in two sections, a north (upper) section and a south (lower) section. The CCC camp headquarters and maintenance buildings were in the north section, and on the south side were the administration building, mess hall, recreation hall, and five barracks. The buildings on the south side were arranged in an oval with three barracks on one side, and two barracks and the recreation hall on the other side with the latrine in the center.

CONSTRUCTION

Unlike the NP-2 tent camp, the two Mesa Verde "winter" camps were constructed in the typical rigid army style. The wood buildings were long and narrow, just wide enough for a double tier of bunks on one side, and a narrow aisle down the other. Each of the five barracks was designed to house 40 men. Camps were to be equipped with a large shower room with a solar water heating system and an auxiliary heating plant for bad weather. In addition to the barracks and utility buildings, the camps typically had a large mess hall, commissary, recreation building, officers' quarters, and equipment storage structures.

In August 1934 the *Kiva Krier* reported that the two new camps were to be more "luxurious" than the NP-2 tent camp in Prater Canyon. The newsletter reported that 25 civilian carpenters were already working on the buildings. The materials used for the new camps were all purchased locally and the tradesmen were also from nearby communities. During the construction of NP-5 and NP-6 there was a carpenter strike when someone spread the rumor that the local carpenters were to be replaced by "men from Denver." The rumor proved to be unfounded and the local carpenters were not replaced.

When NP-5 was abandoned in 1942 the Department of the Interior record listed the buildings, sizes, and original costs of construction.

1 Headquarters	137' x 20'	$2,410.23
1 Mess Hall	176' x 20'	3,201.93
1 Recreation Hall	96' x 20'	2,322.27
5 Barracks	112' x 20'	1,970.41
1 Bath House	66' x 20'	1,161.13
1 Garage	20' x 20'	351.85
1 Warehouse & Office	60' x 20'	1,025.07
1 Oil House	15' x 13'	473.28
1 Equipment Shed	120' x 12'	1,431.74
1 Equipment Shed	120' x 23'	1,043.74
		$13,069.38

All buildings were of rigid construction.

In 1934 the army had designed a sturdy building of interchangeable panels that could easily be dismantled and re-constructed. The Mesa Verde camps NP-5 and NP-6 were rigid wood frame but were not built with the interchangeable panels. In 1941 the army rejected a request for an additional CCC site at Mesa Verde and instead selected Mancos for the site of CCC camp NP-13. The Mancos camp was built according to the army's 1934 revision of CCC camp design, with all the buildings of the rigid portable type using interchangeable panels. Wood frame buildings were designed to be more permanent shelters, although all camps were considered "temporary" in that they were designed to be used 18 months or less. Even rigid "permanent" camps were considered to be temporary because the need for CCC crews or for fire control and maintenance in the parks and forests was not considered a permanent assignment and could change and require movement from one area to another based on the changing needs. CCC camps required federal approval to be established, and once established required re-approval for continuance every six months to coincide with the enrollment periods.

ARCHITECTURE

The Mesa Verde CCC buildings are typical of CCC camps – constructed in a rough and inexpensive manner based on the assumption that they would only be used for a temporary period. In the southern section of camp NP-5 in Chapin Mesa the original road still defines the boundary of the camp and small stones embedded in the ground are still present in sufficient numbers to show the various pathways that connected the buildings of the camp.

Only a few of the CCC buildings constructed 72 years ago are still standing at Mesa Verde. In the northern section of NP-5, which was used as the CCC headquarters and maintenance area, four utility buildings, the camp office, two storage sheds, and a gas station remain. Four buildings remain in fairly good condition and are relatively unchanged since their construction.

On the south side only the recreation hall and Barracks #5 remain. Barracks #5 was given the nickname "Jack Gray Warehouse," after a tradesman who stored supplies in the barracks after camp NP-5 was abandoned in 1942. Three of the five original barracks and the mess hall collapsed from the repeated weight of heavy snow that was not cleared from the abandoned buildings. There is no record of what happened to the fifth barracks building that disappeared from the camp. It may have also collapsed under the weight of snow with the lumber removed for building material elsewhere in the park. In 1946 the park superintendent had requested that the abandoned buildings remaining at NP-5 be used to help build much needed additional employee housing in the ever growing park.

The "Jack Gray Warehouse" built in 1934, is long and narrow with a light wood frame covered on the exterior by 8-inch horizontal lap siding. The wood frame building is not painted, the north and south elevations of the building each have 13 awning windows painted green, and on both the east and west side is a green five-panel entry door. The roof was originally covered with only rolled asphalt paper, and corrugated metal sheets have been installed directly over the historic rolled roofing. On the interior, the building has a tongue-in-groove wood floor, Celotex walls, and an open vaulted ceiling with cross ties.

The Historic American Building Survey (HABS) project of 1999 determined that the framing and construction of the barracks show that it was designed as a temporary shelter. Floor dimensions are 112' x 20', framing is 2x4 at four feet on center, and there is no permanent foundation, and no insulation. The foundation consists of a series of three evenly spaced rows of 6-inch-by-6-inch wood posts running the length of the building.

The "Jack Gray" building is currently used by the park for storage and is unsuited for any other use because it is very unstable due to the lack of an adequate foundation. The post foundation and framing are failing, and the building is in danger of collapsing. Vertical supports and structural bracing have been installed by the park service, but these are only temporary fixes and the building is not expected to last much longer without more substantial improvements in stabilization.

The recreation hall is in fair condition and, like Barracks #5, was constructed in 1934. The exterior construction is of 6-inch tongue-in-groove pine planks. Some of the planks are in-kind replacement planks installed in 1980 due to moisture rotting the original planks. The building is T-shaped with a west-facing entryway and small wood porch covered by a shed roof with entrance through a double doorway.

Opposite the main entry door is a large stage that was used for performances during the occupation of the camp by the CCC. On the north interior wall is a large stone fireplace with an in-floor niche for seating; the sunken area around the fireplace was conducive to socializing. The fireplace was constructed in 1935 by the CCC enrollees who used stone from the abandoned Prater Canyon camp. The insignia of the CCC camp NP-5 is embedded in the rock-faced chimney. Opposite the fireplace area on the south side of the hall are the kitchen facilities and bathrooms.

What remains of the CCC camp at Mesa Verde is important historically,

REC HALL

The recreation hall is in such good condition that it is used by the park today for meetings, conferences, social events, and training. It is not used in the winter as the heating is inadequate, and even when used in the summer months portable fans are necessary for ventilation and cooling. The kitchen facilities and the bathrooms are currently functional.

both because of the age of the structures and because of the significance of the CCC era to Mesa Verde and other national parks and forests of the United States. The work projects done by the CCC at Mesa Verde were major improvements to the park and helped carry out the design philosophy for the park that continues to this day.

In addition to the historic buildings of the CCC, the camp location on Chapin Mesa currently houses offices for the Mesa Verde Research Center. There are four "CCC type" barracks buildings and while the buildings replicate the original CCC barracks they are not National Historic Landmarks. Mesa Verde is assessing the feasibility of preserving the CCC camp's landscape features, the "Jack Gray Warehouse" and the recreation hall. The assessment is studying the possible alternatives for the two buildings.

As barracks #5 is structurally unsafe it might be found that the only alternative is to remove it, or it might be possible to stabilize and rehabilitate the barracks for public use. The recreation hall is being used in good weather and it may be possible to rehabilitate the building for year-round public use. The landscape features can be preserved by continuing the present preservation maintenance. If the buildings were to be converted to public use, parking accommodations would need to be added while preserving the original camp landscape.

(Susana Jones is a senior at Fort Lewis College, majoring in Southwest Studies and Heritage Preservation. In 2004, she worked as an intern for Don Corbeil, historical architect at Mesa Verde.)

1942
AMERICA

A date which will live in infamy," as Franklin Roosevelt described it, took America from isolation into the world. The attack on Pearl Harbor December 7, 1941, brought the United States into World War II, with an unshakable determination to win.

In the next six months, Americans despondently watched as one defeat followed another, particularly in the Pacific theater against the Empire of Japan, which had launched the attack that drove America into the war. Guam and Wake Island fell, along with Hong Kong and Singapore, and the Japanese marched elsewhere, seemingly unstoppable. In early 1942, a pervasive gloom overtook Americans, particularly after the Philippines surrendered in May.

... AS WAR SETTLED OVER THE LAND, THE COUNTRY FINALLY

PULLED OUT OF THE DEPRESSION.

Then came a dramatic reversal, with the Battle of Midway, June 3-6. The American navy handed the Japanese a stunning naval defeat. The latter's advance across the Central Pacific was halted. Never again would they be able to resume the offensive, although many Americans did not comprehend what had just happened.

At the same time, as war settled over the land, the country finally pulled out of the depression. Military-related expenditures had leaped in 1940-41 as the United States tried to strengthen itself, while the rest of the world plunged into war beginning in 1939. Industrial production increased, farm income went up, business improved, jobs appeared, and for the first time in over a decade Americans found opportunities available to rebuild their lives. America geared for a wartime economy even before it marched into conflict.

Times were desperate in 1942, just as they had been in 1932. This time, however, the world situation vexed Americans and generated fears for the future. In contrast, they found their economic situation improving noticeably, while the war impacted their personal lives.

1942
MESA VERDE

Mesa Verde National Park during the Second World War was "on hold," so to speak, with gas rationing, overtime and long work weeks, plus wartime needs and activities that cut into tourism. Visitation numbers collapsed back to where they had been 20 years before and they remained low into 1945.

Staff problems also appeared, as men went off to war. For example, starting in the fall of 1942 the entrance station was unmanned and closed. This led a superintendent to observe that "most visitors ignored or paid slight heed to the informational instructions posted." The stabilization program also suffered, as material and labor went to more urgent needs.

One war-related issue came to haunt Jesse Nusbaum, who returned as acting superintendent during World War II. There were some individuals who wanted the park opened to grazing. He forcefully stated: "The concept of a national park – *for the benefit and enjoyment of all the people*" would not be derailed by local ranchers dressed in patriotism. It was not. The cattle grazed elsewhere.

One bright aspect appeared, however, during these years. The interpretive "force is able to establish closer and more frequent contact with each visitor." The short-handed staff, as it was, tried to "maintain" its "long established prestige for service."

1942
Civilian Conservation Corps

The CCC proved to be one of the most popular, and successful, of the New Deal agencies. In fact, it has been called "the most favorably received of any of the New Deal relief activities." At its peak strength in 1935, it had 500,000 young men on its rolls, and, by the time it ended, more than 2½ million had passed through its ranks. Besides the camps at Mesa Verde, more than 1,500 others spanned the United States.

This "pet" project of President Roosevelt not only was well-liked, but many came to regard it as a permanent American institution. That was not to be. The coming of the draft and then the wartime boom, with its myriad of jobs beckoning, found the youth of the land no longer "rootless" and thus ended the need for the CCC. On June 30, 1942, the agency was allowed to die for lack of a congressional appropriation.

The CCC played an especially prominent role in the West. From the prairies to the mountains, there existed both a need and an abundance of public lands, national forests, and state and local parks in which to work. Franklin Roosevelt's dream of helping American youth, one that he promoted even before he became president, proved its worth throughout the region.

The work done at Mesa Verde was similar to that accomplished all through the West in national parks. Obviously, unique projects like the dioramas existed, but generally the young men labored on comparable projects wherever they were.

What was the major contribution of the Civilian Conservation Corps? It was not what they built, or renovated, or reforested, or fought, as significant as those were or became. It was the young men themselves. One unidentified Mesa Verde CCCer wrote in the *Cliff Dweller* (February 22, 1937), that he had received "opportunities in camp" he was not likely to find elsewhere. The CCC provided, he continued, the opportunities to "advance one's education by attending classes" and the chance to "become a skilled tradesman." Where else could he have turned for such opportunities in the tumultuous '30s?

As Coyne Thompson and John McNamara reflected in later years, their experiences in the CCC were a time of growing up. They learned how to cope with the world as adults, and by the time they left, they weren't kids any more. Coyne probably summed up the experience of many when he concluded, "It was a good experience; there wasn't any doubt about it."

APPENDIX:
A WEEK IN THE DINING HALL LIFE OF A CCCer

DATE	BREAKFAST	DINNER	SUPPER
8/27/1936 (NP-5-C)	Cantaloupe Corn flakes Fresh milk French toast Butter, coffee, syrup	Baked sweet potatoes Sweet corn on cob Radishes, green onion Bread, butter Iced tea, sugar cookies	Roast beef Mashed potatoes Combination salad Buttered fresh peas Bread, butter, coffee, cream
8/28/1936	Fresh peaches Cream of wheat Fresh milk Fried eggs Bread, butter Coffee	Boiled lima beans, bacon Breaded tomatoes Buttered carrots Sliced cucumbers Bread, butter Iced lemonade Raisin pie	Salmon hash Mashed potatoes Spanish sauce Buttered fresh beans Fresh apple sauce Sliced fresh tomatoes Bread, butter, ice water Watermelon
8/29/1936	Grapefruit Corn flakes Bread, butter Scrambled eggs Coffee	Fried hominy Fresh tomatoes Coffee Devil's food cake	Boiled beef & noodles Buttered fresh beans Scalloped cauliflower Bread, butter Coffee, cream
8/30/1936	Cantaloupe Oatmeal, milk French toast, syrup Coffee	Roast fresh pork hams Mashed pots, brn gravy Buttered sweet peas Combination salad Raisin sauce Bread, butter, coffee Canned apricots	Cream of tomato soup Crackers Salmon salad Cold cuts of lunch meat Sliced fresh tomatoes Bread, butter, jam, coffee Watermelon
8/31/1936	Grapefruit, oranges Corn flakes Fresh milk Coffee	Breaded tomatoes Boiled sweet corn on cob Sliced cucumbers Bread, butter, cookies	Roast beef Mashed pots, brn gravy Creamed peas Bread, butter, coffee Mustard
9/1/1936	Stewed prunes Cream of wheat Fresh eggs Fresh milk Biscuits & butter Coffee, sugar	Baked mac & cheese Boiled pinto beans Green onion & radishes Corn bread & butter Iced tea Cherry pie	Boiled beef & noodles Pickled fresh beets Buttered corn Biscuits & butter Coffee
9/2/1936	Cantaloupe Cornmeal mush Hot cakes Syrup Butter, coffee	Boiled lima beans Baked potatoes Combination salad Corn bread Butter, iced buttermilk	Meat loaf Mashed potatoes Brown gravy Radishes & green onions Butter, bread, coffee Fresh milk Pastry, Tapioca pudding

A Note on Sources

John A. Salmond's *The Civilian Conservation Corps, 1933-1942: A New Deal Case Study* (Durham: Duke University Press, 1967) remains the best overall discussion of the CCC. He focused upon the national issues that affected the CCC and its leaders. John C. Paige's *The Civilian Conservation Corps and the National Park Service, 1933-1942: An Administrative History* (National Park Service, U.S. Department of the Interior, 1985) provides an overview of the CCC activities and accomplishments in the National Park Service. Ricardo Torres-Reyes also discusses the impact of New Deal programs on the park in *Mesa Verde National Park, an Administrative History, 1906-1970. Mesa Verde National Park: Shadows of the Centuries*, by Duane A. Smith, discusses the CCC within the entire span of history of Mesa Verde.

Students of the Civilian Conservation Corps in Mesa Verde National Park must begin with the park service records for the CCC which have been preserved in the Research Center, as well as the superintendents' records, which were housed in the park headquarters. In addition, there are selected reports by ECW or CCC inspectors who visited the Mesa Verde Companies 861 and 1843 in response to complaints. These documents can be found in the Camp Inspection Reports, 1933-1942, Colorado; Division of Investigations, Records of the Civilian Conservation Corps, Records Group 33, National Archives. Mesa Verde National Park has an extensive collection of interviews from a CCC oral history project, which was consulted heavily for this work. Cortez, Mancos, and Durango newspapers from the CCC period also contain helpful information.

Additionally, Ron Brown owes a debt of gratitude to enrollees who shared their recollections of their days in the CCC with him. Those with whom he spoke in the early 1990s are Carl Armstrong, Ross Durant, Luis R. Gomez, Hal Gould, Harold Greenlee, Meredith Guillet, Bonifacio Muniz, Mrs. Kenneth Ross, George Stithen, G. Coyne Thompson, Jack Vinger, Henry Vining, Charles M. Watson, Arthur Wilson, and Paul E. Witt. Their recollections of life in Camps NP-5-C and NP-6-C added immeasurably to his understanding of the ways in which this experience affected and even transformed the CCC boys of the 1930s.

Ron would be remiss if he did not acknowledge the very special support of Superintendent Robert Heyder, who took particular interest in his research and permitted him to live in temporary housing in the park while he launched this research on the CCC.

INDEX

Townsend, James W. 4, 41, 46, 48
Trotter, Fred 41
Twain, Mark 25

W-Y

Wagner, Herman 12, 14, 18-19
Watson, Don 14, 60-61
Wetherill Mesa fire 15, 29, 42
White Dog site 59
Wickiup fire 92
Wild Horse Mesa fire 92
Wilson, Arthur 75
winter 12, 31-32, 46, 49, 99
winter camps 115
World War II 100-101, 123-124
Yellowhorse, Sam 53